Empowerment Parenting

How to Raise Resilient Children Who Become Happy, Self-Reliant Adults

Stephanie L. Mann

To order additional copies of this book, contact:
Xlibris
1-888-795-4274
www.Xlibris.com
Orders@Xlibris.com
783006

Empowerment Parenting
A Ten-Step Interactive Guide
Stephanie L. Mann

To Help Youth Develop Self-Esteem and
Stay Centered, Safe, and Healthy

Avoid Drugs, Violence, and Self-Destructive Behavior

Discover the Power of Courage, Character, and Conscience

And Open the Door to Success

138 Interactive Stories, Exercises, and Safety Tips

To families who want to empower their children!

What you can do to help your children grow into resilient, self-reliant, safe, healthy adults.

Freedom and compassion grow when we teach children the power of the human spirit!

Contents

Part 1
Empowerment Parenting for Preteens and Teenagers

Part 2

Empowerment Parenting Guide for Parents and Adults

Stephanie's Story

I was abandoned in Mexico City at age fifteen and didn't speak the language.

As I was growing up, my mother's inheritance allowed us many privileges, but my father felt inadequate and became an alcoholic. My sister was a star pupil, but my brother was the fall guy for my parents' conflicts. They divorced for the second time when I was ten.

A new man moved in before I turned thirteen. He was a Washington DC lobbyist, and he took control of my mother's money and our lives. He persuaded her to move to Mexico City. At age fifteen, I'd had one year of high school and was told I didn't need a private school because my grades were not up to par. I was enrolled at Mexico City College to study Spanish and art. They told college administrators I was eighteen and a high school graduate.

Once I was in college, my mother and her boyfriend flew back to Washington saying they had important business and promised to return within two weeks. She paid a month's rent for a room with a Mexican family for me and left. When the month was up and they didn't return, my landlady threatened to evict me.

Panic set in! I didn't know which way to turn. I had no friends, no family, no one to advise me, and I didn't speak Spanish.

One afternoon, after taking the bus back to my rented room, I saw a small church. The door was open, and I went in. Fear and loneliness overwhelmed me. My family had never attended church, but my grandmother had said, "If you have a problem, turn to God and ask for help." When I left the church, I had a plan.

I talked to the dean of women, and she suggested I become a guide for American tourists. That idea terrified me! I protested saying that my Spanish was terrible. She said, "Americans can't speak it at all. Just do some homework and guide tourists around the city." She handed me a stack of sightseeing books.

Fortunately, a fellow student suggested her Uncle Jose, a cabdriver, might help. It wasn't long before I was showing Americans the sights. I discovered that telling tourists I was abandoned, I received bigger tips.

A couple claimed they were writing a book and asked if Jose and I would take them on a tour of the houses of prostitution. He offered to triple our pay. I hesitated, but Jose said we would take them on a trip they would never forget.

We started at 10:00 p.m. at high-class houses of prostitution and ended up at 4:00 a.m. with older women offering sex for centavos ("Pennies on the dollar"). The husband talked to the women, and when he returned to the table, his wife took notes. We heard horror stories of rape, pimps, abandonment, pregnancy, and girls running away from home because of molestation and abuse.

By the time I got back to my room, I was sick to my stomach. What would happen to me if my mother didn't return? I had heard stories of girls as young as thirteen, forced into prostitution.

I stopped eating and sleeping. My landlady was going to evict me; however, when I became extremely ill, she called a doctor and the dean of women. I didn't know where to find my mother, but I told them about her Washington DC boyfriend. Eventually, the dean located her.

I woke up to find my mother standing over me. I thought I was dreaming. It had been three months, and the doctor told her I might have a venereal disease, which was false and shocking to me. She made immediate arrangements at a hospital in Texas. The problem was the authorities might not let us back into the United States with me in my condition. My mother and the doctor decided we should fly to Nuevo Laredo, Mexico, without luggage. We bought a few trinkets and a large hat to cover my face. We tried to look like tourists and crossed the border into the United States. We rented a car and drove to the hospital in San Antonio, Texas.

After many tests, the doctor stated that I was malnourished and starving to death. Within a week, my health greatly improved. I now had a different perspective and saw my mother through new eyes. I knew she couldn't help herself, and I wasn't angry. My experience was painful and lonely, but in retrospect, I discovered my identity and my values, and I learned to rely on my higher power to survive. I felt sorry for my mother for the choices she had made. I realized she had become a heavy drinker and smoker while living the Washington DC social life.

I attended a variety of colleges before my age and lack of education were discovered, including Colorado College and the University of Southern California. I was expelled from the University of Arizona when they discovered I didn't have a high school diploma and entered Eastern Arizona Junior College to take high school courses.

I received my high school diploma at Pasadena City College, where I met a US Air Force veteran and college student Douglass Mann. We were married when I was eighteen. My mother refused to attend our wedding because I was "marrying below my station in life." Today, we are still together and have raised three successful children. We now have seven grandchildren and six great-grandchildren.

Life can be a difficult journey, but the struggle is our teacher! When we rely on our inner wisdom for guidance and take full responsibility for our future, without anger, we can learn not only to survive but also how to thrive.

Preface

Empowerment Parenting was written to support parents, guardians, and teachers. The mixed messages in American society can confuse impressionable youth. Adults can help youth unleash their potential to succeed. Empowered children can discover they have the inner strength to resist temptation and avoid self-destructive behaviors. When we teach youth to listen to their inner wisdom and pay attention to their intuition and instincts, they will develop a self-protective conscience, which helps them take responsibility for their own behavior.

It is easier to prevent self-destructive behavior than to change behavior after bullies affect children or they turn to drugs, misuse sex, or develop other destructive behaviors.

Children are born with a healthy conscience and the power to overcome life's challenges regardless of what happens to them. They can grow stronger and make the *maturity flip*. Youth can discover their "spiritual center" as they rise above difficult experiences. In the process, they can see a new reality for their life.

As a crime and violence prevention specialist for thirty-nine years, my goal is to share what I learned from my experience. I discovered why many youth succeed while others struggle and fail to reach their potential.

Self-accomplishment gives children the greatest reward! When youth grow from within, they realize they have the power to stay safe and healthy.

(Many abused, neglected, and homeless adults shared their problems and success stories, which are included in this book. Graphics are enclosed to make the ten steps easier to understand. Young people are fountains of wisdom when parents take the time to listen and share stories, which can help to empower them.)

Help and Support for Youth and Adults

America has an epidemic of bullies, domestic violence, child abuse, drugs, gangs, and gun violence. Consider starting a support group to help hurting people heal. Discuss one step at a time with youth, troubled families, and homeless adults in a social, church, or civic group. Offering support to individuals and families can change their lives and help them stay centered, safe, and healthy.

What People Are Saying about *Empowerment Parenting*

Empowerment Parenting reflects the over forty years of research by the author, Mrs. Stephanie Mann, a crime and violence prevention consultant. She has inspired, mentored, and provided resources and information that has helped many in my neighborhood with violence prevention and intervention in Richmond, California. The invaluable information contained in this book *Empowerment Parenting* you will not find anywhere else. I guarantee it.

—A. J. Jelani, President, Peace On The Streets Org., Inc. San Francisco, California

Empowerment Parenting is a must-read for everyone who deals with children. Parents, teachers, and coaches alike will find the step-by-step training programs provided can restore self-value in youth; decrease or stop bullying, crime, and violence; and put young lives on a positive, self-fulfilling track. Everyone knows a child. Everyone needs this book.

—Rebecca Kimbel, TV producer and speaker, Eureka, California

I couldn't put this book down! In my opinion, every community, church, family, and school should have this book. Once it's read, it changes how you view a child, and it allows you to see why adult problems exist. Teaching a child how to know their self-worth and purpose was a wake-up call for my students. I taught this book in Jr. High and High School. Without a doubt, this book will help you in your journey to strengthen your family and help stop the social isolation that fuels domestic violence, abuse, gangs, and other destructive behaviors.

—Deborah Faith Taylor, President/Founder of Wings of Love, Memphis, Tennessee

The answer to "It takes a village." This book is so well written and easy to understand. I really believe it needs to be part of our public school curriculum. So many dysfunctional families are looking for answers. This book has so many useful and easily applied ideas to make everyone's life better!

—Lynda Brown, Retired in Henderson, Nevada

A truly educational, encouraging read and ride, leading us from darkness to light, from suppression to liberty.

—Rev. R. Geoffrey Brown, MDiv, ThM, PhD

This guide is an excellent book for all. Stephanie teaches you how to deal with the challenges of life in a way that makes it easy for any person to decide to make choices that positively impact their own life and the lives of those around them. This is a must-read.

—Sher Graham, EVP, NeuroBehavior, The Synergy Solutions Group, Mobile, Alabama

Empowerment Parenting will make a significant contribution toward the prevention of youth violence.

—Warren Rupf, former Contra Costa County Sheriff, California

As an educator and parent, I can enthusiastically ascertain that *Empowerment Parenting* is a superb resource in helping parents and teachers help their children be victors in life. To be healthy, resilient, and whole, young people have to know how to successfully navigate the ever-increasing obstacles along the way. Stephanie Mann has been able to do just that, having distilled the many decades of her experience as a crime prevention specialist into this book of wisdom, an easy read, yet deeply insightful. I wholeheartedly recommend *EP*!

—David Rosenblum, Special Education Teacher, Fremont, California, Unified School District

Acknowledgments

I am indebted to my friends Ann Berens, Gretchen Brambach, and Rev. J. W. Rueb for their advice and wisdom. Thanks to my special friend Mary Claire Blakeman for her editorial skills. Additional guidance and support came from Jim Becker, executive director of the Center for Human Development; Contra Costa County Assemblywoman Lynne C. Leach; Contra Costa County Sheriff Warren Rupf; Oakland City Manager Robert C. Robb; and Oakland Assistant City Manager Ellis Mitchell. Thanks to Child Assault Prevention for letting us reprint the "No, Go, Yell, Tell" technique.

Don Marx, executive director of Community Peacemakers, has contributed immeasurably to the making of this book. He has also offered steadfast encouragement on the direction and vision for the Street Safe Kids program.

Thanks to computer experts Heather Bianchi and John Muth for their patience and assistance. Thanks to the young people and students Ali Hook, Gina Harezlak, Aimee McIntire, and Christian Jacobson for their wise thoughts, which we have added to this text.

This book would not have been possible without the dedicated community activists in the Bay Area who shared their volunteer experiences. They include Mary Ann Wright of the Mary Ann Wright Foundation; Pastor Flemon Henry from New Saint Paul's Baptist

Church; A. J. Jelani, executive director of Peace on the Streets; Fred Jackson, program director, North Richmond Neighborhood House; and Diego Garcia, director of Telpochcalli for abused children.

A big thank-you to my friends Harry Miller and John and Marge Minney for their support and faith in this project. And last but not least, thank you to my husband, who has been my mentor, adviser, and cheerleader for over forty years. Without his love, encouragement, patience, and culinary skills, this book would not have been possible.

Thank you Xlibris Publishing Co. for your professional guidance in updating the *Street Safe Kids Guidebook* and *Empowerment Parenting*.

To all of them, I express my deepest thanks for the time and support so generously given.

How to Use This Guide

Empowerment Parenting is an interactive guide that has been written to help preteens, teenagers, and young adults avoid self-destructive behavior. This ten-step tool offers parents and adults new ways to help teens grow up safe, secure, and centered from within so they can reach their potential.

By using this guide, you can share positive values and awaken a teen's self-awareness. A self-aware teen is more mature and more likely to make positive choices. Learning these steps early in life can help teens build on a strong foundation of character and courage to reach their full potential.

We suggest teens read one step a week along with an adult adviser. Or teens can read the steps by themselves, depending on age. Adults should also set aside a specific time each week to talk about each step in order to open the door to positive discussions. The reader will need a notebook and adult encouragement to complete the self-awareness exercises and the review after each step. Included with this guide are additional ways to reinforce each step (see part 2, "Empowerment Parenting Guide for Parents and Adults").

This ten-step guide can also be used with neighborhood, youth, civic, and religious-discussion groups. A facilitator can open up opportunities for group discussion so participants can share personal life experiences. Graphics, illustrations, and true stories are provided to help teens understand why this journey to become self-aware is a worthwhile venture.

What Does the Word *Spiritual* Mean in This Guide?

The single greatest threat to our teenagers' future is the failure to teach them how to find inner power and strength. True inner power can be found within every human spirit. This lack of understanding is reflected in the extreme behavior of teenagers involved in drugs, gangs, hate groups, cults, addictions, shootings, murder, and suicide. The growing trend is to lie, cheat, and abuse others or to misuse drugs and sex without understanding the consequences.

Lack of self-awareness, or spiritual ignorance, is the largest social problem we face today. We cannot legislate character or morality, but we can offer our teenagers a spiritual path to self-awareness so they develop both self-esteem and compassion for others. More than 90 percent of people in the United States believe in a higher power, a spiritual power that is greater than any human effort. Further, half of that group belongs to a religious faith where families find support and a community that helps individuals to modify negative behavior.

While this book *does not* advocate any specific religious belief or discipline, it nevertheless *does* point to the existence of a spiritual reality that underpins our lives. In these pages, you will see references to a *higher power*, an *inner wisdom*, or the *Creator's laws*. Those words mean different things to different people.

In the context of this book, however, one of the most important things for teens to understand is that we are all spiritual beings with a conscience, intuition, and instincts to protect us, if we choose to listen. We can pay attention to the dictates of the conscience and cultivate positive spiritual influences, or we can ignore it and succumb to negative influences.

We are either growing in self-control and developing self-awareness or becoming ego-centered as we disregard our impact on others.

Every teenager is a unique human being with the potential to develop the three Cs—that is, courage, character, and conscience. The following lists contain traits of the three Cs that will help you and the teens in your life better understand what it means to become a self-aware and street-safe person.

By developing these attributes, young people will have an opportunity to reach their fullest potential and to truly define the word *spiritual* in the best sense.

Courage	Character	Conscience
Does the right thing	Positive attitude	Does unto others …
Confident	Resilient	Guided by a higher power
Brave and fearless	Honest, sincere	Conflict; opportunity to grow
Challenges self	Doesn't need credit	Controls self, not others
Stands up for self	Speaks up for others	Feels remorse
Stays calm no matter what	Listens to others	Knows right from wrong
Can admit failure	Says "I'm sorry"	Has inner wisdom
Can walk away	Patient	Doesn't condemn others
Volunteers to help	Finds the good in others	Can handle anger calmly
Takes a leadership role	Truthful	Can forgive others

As they go through the steps of this book, teens will have numerous opportunities to evaluate their progress in becoming more attuned to their conscience. Readers can refer to the preceding lists at any time, or the reader and adult adviser may want to add their own terms that best define these positive traits.

What Makes a Resilient, Happy Child?

(From the Author's Experience)

I started working in my community and eventually became a crime-prevention coordinator in high-fear neighborhoods. I saw drug abuse, domestic violence, child abuse, and social decay, but at the same time, I saw children who were able to move beyond abuse and fear and excel in their chosen fields.

I asked myself why some children fail to cope with life while others excel under similar conditions. I found that answer when I worked with the homeless and started a men's support group. Men, including ex-felons, wanted to know what they needed to change to get off drugs and to stay out of prison. A church leader and a group of homeless men shared their stories about growing up with abuse. I shared with them what I told my children. Within three months, four men had found jobs and two men admitted they had drug problems. We got them into drug rehab. That was a small success, considering we started out with twenty-one men, but we all learned a great deal from one another.

As a result, I've seen the critical need to help strengthen families when children are young. That is why I've developed this ten-step guidebook. It teaches what many men and women never learned in their homes. It is a guide to help you find answers for your family.

The key is self-awareness, which leads to self-discipline, self-control, and self-esteem. No matter what chaos has occurred in their lives, the youth have a good chance to succeed if they develop the three Cs (courage, character, and conscience) and become self-motivated. When youth have the emotional tools to help them avoid anger and temptations, they grow strong from within and are less likely to go down a self-destructive path.

Adults can help a child learn to stay spiritually centered and become street safe.

All "A Life Experience" stories are true! They are from experiences of the author, her family, or the people she has worked with for forty years. The names have been changed to protect their identities.

Part 1

Empowerment Parenting for Preteens and Teenagers

This section helps parents and other adults work with youth to strengthen their inner power of self-discipline, self-control and self-esteem. Empowering youth reduces self-destructive behaviors, which can keep them safe and healthy.

Step 1

Recognize How Special You Are

As you start out in life, you may not realize you are unique in every way. No one else has your smile, fingerprints, hidden talents, or ability to see the world as you do. Just as no two snowflakes are exactly alike, no two people are the same. Among billions of people on earth, no one else has your DNA. You are an extraordinary creation. You have a brain more complicated than any computer, and you have an inner passion that you need to discover. You also have the ability to rise above any limitations to realize your dreams.

The first step in being street safe is to recognize just how unique and special you are—because you are someone who is worth protecting. When you really let this fact sink in, you can see that self-esteem comes from within and is not dependent on anyone or anything else outside of you. Grown-ups and other teenagers can let you down and disappoint you, but when you learn to trust the spiritual power within yourself, you will find inner

You are an extraordinary human being.

strength. And when you have the self-awareness to realize what a special being you are, you will no longer be an easy target for anyone who wants to put you down or hurt you, whether it's someone close to you or a stranger on the street.

A. Learn to Cope with Ups and Downs

Some days, you may feel good, and it seems as though your self-esteem is up. Other days, you may feel down and wonder where your self-worth has gone. These feelings are normal as you learn to stretch and grow stronger. Life is a roller-coaster ride of ups and downs. Anyone can handle the good days. What's important is how you handle the days when nothing goes right. Learning how to cope when things aren't going your way is part of the life lessons you must learn. It's called *character development*. It's important also to remember that even if your feelings go up and down, your self-esteem doesn't have to. That's because your self-esteem comes from within, and it grows when you recognize and remember how unique and special you are.

A Life Experience

Colin was an excellent swimmer who enjoyed the sport and got praised for his abilities at the pool. But at school, he didn't have the same kind of winning confidence. He would fumble the football, and several boys would make fun of him for his lack of skill on the field. He also couldn't write as well as some students could. Colin was sometimes teased, and he often felt stupid. His mother told him to focus on the things he did well and reminded him that he would improve in the areas where he wasn't so strong.

But Colin pouted and said he was going to punch out the next person who made fun of him. His mother said that wasn't the way to win friends or to feel better. She also pointed out that he couldn't change the behavior of others, but he could work harder, concentrate on his strengths, and learn to laugh at himself and ignore the teasing.

Questions to Consider

What do you think Colin is feeling? Is hitting someone his only option? What else can Colin do? Do you think he will continue to pout, or will he follow his mother's advice?

B. Protect Your Self-Worth

As important as it is, simply recognizing how special you are is not enough. You must also see that you are worth protecting. You may have to defend yourself against those who try to take away your self-esteem, as you'll see in the discussions that follow.

1. Don't let family members confuse you.

You may want to think of yourself as unique; however, it's hard to feel special when you are given orders to follow and no one seems to listen to you. Parents and caretaking relatives may mean well, but they may also be critical. For example, they can say things like "Don't eat so much," "Stand up straight," "That skirt is too short," "You look like a bum," "Look at me when I'm talking to you," "Don't talk to me like that," "Why do you hang around with that bunch?" and "Can't you do anything right?" Adult family members may treat you as if you don't have feelings or a mind of your own. Often, they see themselves as bosses, teachers, or dictators, and they may forget to listen to your side of the story. That

Don't let anyone throw you off balance.

doesn't mean it is right. It means you need to know how to handle it. Parents and other grown-ups are not perfect, but many of them try to do their best. Sometimes, they are simply passing on to you the things that their parents taught them. The key is to remember you are unique and special, no matter what anyone says—parents included.

2. Don't let a family breakup shake you.

The breakup of a family can throw anyone off center, and it can be especially confusing to children and teenagers. Parents can say angry things about each other. One parent may try to persuade you that he or she is right and the other parent is wrong. You may find yourself in a different role where you have to take a parent's position instead of your rightful place as the child. Or you may be the peacemaker or the star that everyone expects you to be. Perhaps you are the troublemaker or a problem kid whom everyone blames. Family breakups can make you feel moody, angry, shy, depressed, or less confident. Your school grades may drop, or you may think about taking drugs to feel good again. Your self-esteem may fall, but if you handle it right, you can grow stronger.

3. Don't accept bullying from peers and friends.

Besides your family, friends and peers can give you confusing messages as well. Children and teenagers can tease and bully. It's hard to feel special if you don't fit in or feel rejected. We all want to be loved. Growing up is especially painful if classmates use put-downs because you don't wear the right clothes or you have a disability. Or you may feel too tall, too thin, too short, or too fat. You can even be put down for being too smart or the teacher's pet. Being subjected to taunts or bullying is unfair, but it's common when children or teenagers lack maturity. Just remember, you have incredible potential if you keep your sense of humor and practice patience and self-awareness.

4. Don't be intimidated by rude adults.

Adults outside your family can also be thoughtless or cruel. A neighbor can yell at you for something as simple as kicking a ball over his or her fence. A waiter, shopkeeper, or clerk may ignore you in favor of waiting on an adult. Adults may even push ahead of you in lines at the movies or grocery. These situations are opportunities to practice being patient and speaking up calmly. You will grow stronger.

5. Don't let drugs or violence rob you of your self-worth.

When you lack inner strength and awareness of your unique identity, other people can spark your anger. That makes it easier for you to be attracted to violence or escape into drugs. When you feel bad about yourself, your next move may be to join a group to smoke pot, drink alcohol, have sex, or bully someone. You may temporarily get high or feel better when you use drugs or alcohol or vent anger through violence, but the high will not last, and you will end up in worse shape than before. So you may take drugs or some other escape to get away from feeling bad about yourself. That can lead you into a vicious cycle in which the things you do for a quick fix stop working. The only way out is to learn to respect and appreciate yourself and value your body. Don't let anyone or anything violate your health. Others may try to pull you down and convince you that you are not special, but you can grow stronger if you protect and value your self-worth.

A Life Experience

Ernestina lived in a high-crime neighborhood when her mother died of cancer. Her parents had always wanted her to go to college, so Ernestina worked hard to get good grades. She learned to rely on faith to heal from the grief of losing her mother. She spent her free time teaching younger children how to use a computer at the local library.

One day, a school counselor who loved her attitude asked her why she was so happy even though her outward circumstances were difficult. Ernestina thought for a moment and answered, "My mother and dad made me feel special, and they taught me to work hard and be a blessing in other people's lives."

C. Remember, You Are Unique and Special

Webster's Dictionary defines the word *special* as "distinguished by some unusual quality, being designed for a special purpose." Problems arise when we forget how special we are or rely only on the opinions of others. All of us are imperfect, but we are still special. Human beings struggle to become self-aware and self-confident. Perhaps you have heard the expression "God doesn't make junk." The fact is you are unique in every way. Don't give anyone the power to change your attitude from positive to negative. Reach for your higher self. You have a responsibility to discover your inner power so you can live a healthy, productive life. No one can do it for you. Self-esteem is a do-it-yourself project.

D. Build Your Self-Esteem

To launch your self-esteem-building project, you may wish to use the following two suggestions, or you can move on to section E, "Exercise in Self-Awareness," for more insights on the task ahead.

1. Follow your dreams.

Put down all electronic devices. Take the time to dream about your future and to appreciate life. In the summer, lie down on the grass and visualize what you want to accomplish. In the spring, sit by a pond or stream and renew your dreams for your life. In the fall and winter, enjoy a warm fire or bundle up in a blanket and let your imagination help you discover your passion. Write in a journal or draw pictures of your ideal future. No matter how you do it, you are worth the time it takes to explore your hopes and dreams.

2. Read an inspirational book or see an uplifting movie.

Movies and books affect us more than we think they do. When you read or see the story of someone who has overcome tough situations, it can inspire you to do the same. For example, read *The Story of My Life* by Helen Keller, or see the movie *The Miracle Worker*. Helen was born deaf and blind but achieved great success. At age eight, she could only grunt, scream, and point in frustration as she grabbed food off her parents' plates. She was deaf and blind. Her family thought she was intellectually disabled and discussed putting her in an institution. As a last resort, a teacher, Anne Sullivan, was hired to see if Helen could learn. Love translated into tough discipline, and it transformed Helen. She learned to read, write, and speak and became a world-famous writer and lecturer.

Questions to Consider

What do you think made the difference in Helen's life? Write out your answer. Or finish this sentence: Helen Keller's story would not have happened if _____. You and your friends may also want to see other inspirational movies that are true stories about the power of the human spirit, such as *Patch Adams*, *My Left Foot*, *Stand by Me*, or *Rudy*.

E. Exercise Your Self-Awareness

The step-1 exercises presented here can help you see what you need in order to grow into the secure and street-safe person you want to be. Do each exercise, and then talk with a parent or adult adviser about what you've discovered.

Exercise A: Measure Your Progress

Just as a real barometer can indicate the condition of the weather, so too can the *attitude barometers* in these exercises help you see the condition of your self-esteem.

a. Attitude Barometer 1

How do you feel about yourself today? Check out the attitude barometer at the end of this chapter (Step 1: Exercise A). This barometer is your personal evaluation so you can discover where you are and where you want to be in ten weeks, six months, or two years. *Read* the barometer, and *circle* the statement that is closest to how you feel about yourself. Everyone has good and bad days, but we all have a deep-down feeling about who we are and how we fit into the family, school, neighborhood, and community. Now that you have circled where you are today, *underline* the statement that is closest to where you want to be in two months. This choice can represent your immediate goal. As you go through each of the ten steps, think about what you need to do to accomplish your goal.

b. Attitude Barometer 2

A second attitude barometer can be found at the end of step 10. This barometer is for you to use after you complete each step in the chapters ahead. *Write* one statement, in your own words, that expresses your attitude after completing each step. You may feel the same as you did when you completed barometer no. 1, or you may feel differently. In this way, you can see for yourself the progress you are making. Your goal is to work your way up as you grow stronger and develop self-esteem. No matter where you are on the first barometer, your goal is to eventually reach your unlimited potential.

Exercise B: Use the Self-Evaluation Checklist

Read the statements on the following self-evaluation checklist for teens. Think carefully about your response to each statement. Circle the number that best describes your evaluation of yourself, with 1 indicating strong *dis*agreement and 5 indicating strong *agree*ment. For example, consider the statement "I handle anger in a calm and constructive way." If that's really true for you, circle the number 5 on the "Strongly Agree" side of the columns, but if you lash out and hurt others when you are angry, circle the number 1. Add up all the numbers when you complete the list. If you circle all 1s, your score will be 20, and if you circle all 5s, it will be 100. If your score is under 40, consider discussing the results with a trusted adult. In two months, do this exercise again to evaluate how you are growing. The higher the numbers, the more you value yourself and others. Be honest with yourself so you can grow in self-confidence and self-discipline, which is the best way to build the self-esteem you deserve to enjoy as the special and unique person you are!

Step 1: Exercise B

Self-Evaluation Checklist for Teens

	Strongly Disagree				Strongly Agree
I feel special and self-confident most of the time.	1	2	3	4	5
I show respect for all my family members.	1	2	3	4	5
I get along well with my peers.	1	2	3	4	5
I handle anger in a calm and constructive way.	1	2	3	4	5
If a friend betrays a confidence, I can speak up calmly.	1	2	3	4	5
I am involved in school to improve my confidence.	1	2	3	4	5
I willingly take on new challenges.	1	2	3	4	5
If I don't agree with my peers, I can say no.	1	2	3	4	5
I think before I speak in anger.	1	2	3	4	5
I can walk away if someone tries to bully me.	1	2	3	4	5
I don't need to be invited to a party to feel good.	1	2	3	4	5
I am learning to handle rejection.	1	2	3	4	5

If I feel overwhelmed, I share my feelings with others.	1	2	3	4	5
I listen to friends without judgment, and I don't gossip.	1	2	3	4	5
I feel comfortable when I meet new people.	1	2	3	4	5
In a crisis, I can stay calm, cool, and collected.	1	2	3	4	5
I can take direction from authority (officials, police, teachers).	1	2	3	4	5
I take the time to do something special for others.	1	2	3	4	5
I have identified areas I need to improve on.	1	2	3	4	5
I make good decisions to improve my life.	1	2	3	4	5

My points add up to

F. Review

What did you learn about yourself and about other people in this step?

_____

_____

What did you learn from this step that made you feel better about yourself?

_____

_____

Now, add a statement to your barometer at the end of step 10.

Once you have completed the reading and exercises for this step, both you and an adult adviser should sign below. By doing so, you are solidifying your commitment to growing stronger and safer.

Adult Adviser's Signature _____

Reader's Signature _____

Stay strong through the hard times. Keep a positive attitude.

—Aimee, aged eighteen

Attitude Barometer #1

Instructions

Read the following statements, and circle those that best represent how you feel about yourself today.

True power comes from within.
I am self-aware and use self-control
to find my higher purpose

I am unique in every way.
I have talents to be discovered.

I want to improve my self-awareness,
self-control and my relationships

I am learning how to handle pain
and anger so I am in control of me.
relationships.

Life can be difficult and painful.
I blame others for my problems.

An adult makes me angry. I won't be
controlled or ignored. I make bad
choices just to show him or her I can
make my own choices.

I follow my friends because they are
smarter than I am.

I often feel lonely and depressed.

Step 1 – Exercise A

I will be successful. I am taking
responsibility for my future.

I am taking charge of my life. I will
accomplish my goals.

I will find friends to pull me up, not
people who try to knock me down.

I want to be healthy and happy.
What do I need to know?

I feel empty and isolated. I
sometimes take drugs to feel good.

It makes me feel important to put
other people down.

I don't care about others. Nobody
cares about me.

I don't care who I hurt. I don't even
care about me.

Step 2

Discover Strength through Pain

To be street safe and self-aware, you need to understand this basic truth about life: it isn't what happens to us but how we *react* to what happens that determines our character. Our reactions can create more pain for ourselves and for others, or we can act responsibly and learn from the experience. Learning to handle emotional pain is part of growing up. We all go through situations that hurt our feelings, shake our self-esteem, or make us feel worthless. We can grow stronger and more confident when we understand that pain teaches us valuable lessons about ourselves.

So the second step in street-safe awareness is to discover strength through pain. No one should pretend this lesson is easy or that you should ignore your feelings, nor should you make excuses for someone who causes pain for you, such as an abusive person. But you can find strength on the other side of pain. You can grow into a street-safe person who does not inflict pain on yourself or other people. To grow in that direction, you must make the *maturity flip*, which is an important step on the path to self-awareness that you'll learn more about in the section that follows.

A. Make the Maturity Flip to Grow Stronger

The *maturity flip* is the point at which you move from being a self-centered child to becoming a self-aware, mature person. It also means that you take the feelings and opinions of others into account. The mature person develops empathy and reacts calmly and rationally instead of lashing out emotionally or violently.

The maturity flip is the flip from childish behavior and the attitudes of "I want …" and "I don't care about anyone else …" to an attitude that reflects your ability to handle most problems with self-discipline and with concern about how you affect others.

If you are faced with a traumatic situation, such as the death of a parent or a person you love, you may need to flip quickly from childhood to adulthood. Generally, however, becoming mature is a gradual process that takes place over time. Regardless of how you move through this process, you will sooner or later come to a point where you have a choice to make. That choice is whether you will act like a mature person or continue to act childishly. You have the opportunity to make that choice every day of your life.

B. Understand the Stages of Maturity

To help you understand how someone becomes a mature adult, it's useful to remember that all people go through a series of stages during their growth. These stages are outlined in the following.

Stages of Maturity

As you read about the stages of maturity, can you identify your friends or family members—or yourself—in any of them?

Stage 1—*The Baby*

When babies are born, they cry for food, clean diapers, and attention. They are only aware of themselves and have no concern for others.

Stage 2—*The Child*

Children are concerned about their needs but are beginning to become aware of others. If they are taught properly, they learn to share toys, take turns, and refrain from hitting others. Eventually, children recognize that they are not the center of the universe, and they can take the needs of other people into account as they become more mature.

Stage 3—*The Preteen or Teenager*

Teens are becoming self-aware. They are learning to handle most conflicts calmly, to apologize for mistakes, and to take responsibility for their behavior. They are able to solve most personal problems and show sensitivity to the needs of others. They are finding their own identities. This stage is the critical time for teens to develop self-control and to learn to live by their consciences.

Stage 4—*The Adult*

Most adults use self-control to stay cool, calm, and collected. They have learned to be guided by their consciences and to solve their problems rationally. They demonstrate sensitivity to others. They feel remorse for wrongdoing.

C. Don't Delay Your Growth

The maturity flip can be delayed if you don't go through this process and make it past the critical stage of developing self-control as a preteen or teen. If you grow up in a troubled family, you may have a difficult time maturing emotionally. By the same token, an overprotective parent can delay your maturation. If your parent fights your battles for you, then you can become dependent on that parent, and you will lack the skills you need to handle the world.

A neglectful or abusive parent can make you feel unloved or leave you thinking that no one cares for you. As a result, you may turn your feelings outward in anger or inward in depression. If you hold on to resentments about the way a parent, classmate, or relative treats you, you can start down a self-destructive path. Anger and resentment are negative emotions that can pull you down. If you think no one cares about you, then you may care little about others, you can develop a big need for attention, and you may show little or no remorse for hurting others or doing wrong.

In either case, whether parents are overprotective or neglectful and abusive, they can deprive you of the tools you need to manage your own emotions and actions. Such parenting styles can also short-circuit the natural progression of the maturity cycle, and you may remain emotionally stuck. Instead of growing into a responsible adult, you can continue to act like a self-centered child.

When you don't know how to mature properly, your anger can fester and become self-destructive. If you fill your mind with resentments, they can take over your life, making you feel alone and depressed. If you don't learn how to handle pain, you can become either physically violent or emotionally weak—either a person who covers up pain by striking out or one who is fragile and oversensitive. Pain is our teacher, whether we like it or not. So embrace it and learn from it. Seek help from trusted adults who can help you make the maturity flip. Don't let anything delay your emotional growth.

D. Don't Let Drugs or Alcohol Stop Your Progress

Drugs keep young people from maturing properly. By using drugs or alcohol, you temporarily block pain so you cannot become stronger or learn the lesson that the pain is trying to teach you. Since you're temporarily putting off the pain, it will come back—and usually, it's worse. Some teens drink beer or take drugs to feel confident, happy, or acceptable to some group. Drugs keep teens from maturing naturally and learning to be self-confident and can become an emotional crutch. As a result, drugs and alcohol take away self-awareness and self-protective instincts. Drugs give an illusion of self-confidence. Girls may become a victim of rape or other sexual assault. They can become depressed, develop low self-esteem, or get pregnant. Boys may find that drugs lead to angry, abusive, violent, or self-destructive behavior.

The following are statistical facts from the Centers for Disease Control and Prevention (CDC) about drugs and alcohol:– **Alcohol and Public Health**

Fact Sheet - Underage Drinking

Alcohol is the most commonly used and abused drug among youth in the United States.[1]

- Excessive drinking is responsible for more than 4,300 deaths among underage youth each year, and cost the U.S. $24 billion in economic costs in 2010.[2,3]
- Although drinking by persons under the age of 21 is illegal, people aged 12 to 20 years drink 11% of all alcohol consumed in the United States.[4] More than 90% of this alcohol is consumed in the form of binge drinks.[4]
- On average, underage drinkers consume more drinks per drinking occasion than adult drinkers.[5]
- In 2013, there were approximately 119,000 emergency rooms visits by persons aged 12 to 21 for injuries and other conditions linked to alcohol.

Drinking Levels among Youth

The 2017 Youth Risk Behavior Survey found that among high school students, during the past thirty days,

- 30 percent drank some amount of alcohol
- 14 percent binge-drank
- 6 percent drove after drinking alcohol
- 17 percent rode with a driver who had been drinking alcohol

A Life Experience

My mother rebelled against her strict upbringing and her parents' religious restrictions. She wanted to do her own thing, but she couldn't see the consequences of making bad choices as a teenager. She started innocently looking for fun with her friends by drinking and smoking, at age fourteen. She was a talented pianist and writer with a dream to write a book or become a concert pianist. As life's problems developed, she relied on alcohol to cope. Eventually, as she

Reach for your higher purpose

grew older, alcohol turned her into two different people: a loving mother in the morning and, by evening, an angry alcoholic as she pounded the piano, playing tunes she had written in her youth. It took a while for me to realize it, but eventually, I came to understand that my mother's behavior was not her fault. She never developed the self-awareness to reach her goals. She never made the "maturity flip" to become a responsible adult who could handle pain without escaping through alcohol or drugs. During the final weeks of her life, my mother apologized for not being there for her family and regretted the path she had chosen. Due to a lifelong smoking habit, she died from emphysema.

Questions to Consider

What other choices could my friend's mother have made when she was younger? How could she have learned to handle pain in a positive way?

E. Practice Speaking Up

No one enjoys being bullied or having others inflict emotional pain on him or her, but you can grow through it. Practice speaking up! Report negative behavior or walk away from a bad situation. Share how you feel with a trusted friend or an adult who will listen. Think back to step 1 and remember how special you are. Ask your higher power to give you strength and wisdom. Practice handling pain without anger, and you are less likely to be a victim. Solving problems builds self-esteem and helps you develop self-confidence.

A Life Experience

Bobby came home from kindergarten crying because a classmate was punching him. He refused to go back to school. At that time, Superman was the hero of the day. His mother explained that the quiet reporter Clark Kent got stronger when he put on his Superman costume. As he stared at his mother with tears in his eyes, she explained how Superman could bounce bullets off his chest.

She told Bobby he had to learn to bounce *word bullets* off his chest so the bully couldn't upset him. A few days later, he was crying again. His mother told him that crying only made him more vulnerable and repeated how to handle a bully. Several weeks went by. One afternoon, Bobby came running home all excited and said he had taken care of Billy. "What did you do?" his mother asked.

In a triumphant voice, he announced, "When Billy started bullying me, I told him to stop it, or I would punch him in the nose. When he didn't stop, I told my teacher. He leaves me alone now."

Questions to Consider

What did Bobby learn? How can this experience benefit him in the future? What choices will you suggest if a younger child asks you for help?

F. Exercise Your Self-Awareness

Your ability to accept and learn from painful situations is a mark of your maturity. These exercises will help you make an honest evaluation of where you stand currently in terms of handling problems, and they will shed light on what you need to do to reach your goals in the future.

Exercise A: Evaluate Your Maturity

You can tell a lot about your own maturity if you take the time to evaluate it. Answer these questions silently to yourself, or write your answers in your notebook:

- How did you handle your last conflict with a friend? What did you learn about your friend? What did you learn about yourself?
- If you see someone being mistreated, what will you do? If you hear about someone defacing or destroying property, what will you do?
- List the ways you help yourself feel better when you are upset. How do you let go of anger? Can you forgive others and move on?
- Who was the last person you upset, and what happened? Did you apologize for your behavior?

Exercise B: Evaluate Your Relationships and Activities

Are your friends helping you grow into the mature person you want to be? What are you doing to grow stronger when you experience emotional pain? Write down in your notebook this heading: "My Activity List." Next to it, make two columns. Title one column "Productive Activities" and the other "Unproductive Activities." *Productive* refers to an activity that can improve your skills, such as meditating, reading books, playing sports, or finding a hobby. The *unproductive* description applies to a passive or harmful activity that will not improve your future, such as overuse of texting, drinking, smoking, taking drugs, hanging with a gang, or playing video games. By listing your activities, you can help yourself see which activities help you mature and develop skills and which ones cannot.

Now, make another list. Name it "My Friends." List all your friends in these columns, both those you consider part of your productive activities and those on the unproductive side. By making such a list, you can begin to see who is pulling you up and who is not. We all need to think about the friends we choose because they influence our behavior. Are your friends influencing you to participate in activities that are good for you?

Here are some questions to help you decide which list to place your activities and friends in. What do I do in my free time? Do my friends and activities have a positive or negative effect on me? Why do I admire these friends? What lessons have they taught me? As you mature, you will be able to speak up without anger. You can also choose not to participate in negative behavior that can be harmful to you or others. (See the "Step 2: Exercise B" worksheet at the end of this step.)

Exercise C: Evaluate Your Ability to Handle Emotional Pain

Try to see painful situations as a time to grow stronger. When evaluating your self-awareness and maturity, think about how you will handle a variety of situations. Write your answers to these two questions as you consider each situation described here:

How will you react today?
How can you turn a hurtful situation into a learning experience?

- My mother puts me down in front of others. She says I am lazy and fat.
- My father, who lives in another town, promises to pick me up for the weekend, but he doesn't call and doesn't show up.
- I tell a friend a personal confidence, and he or she tells others.
- I hear that someone is spreading rumors about me.
- My favorite jacket is stolen from my locker.
- My girl- or boyfriend breaks up with me.
- I find out my closest friend has told me a big lie.
- My assignment is stolen. I know who took it. I got an incomplete, and he got a B.
- My dream girl or boy asks to sit with me at lunch. Then she or he humiliates me.
- My classmates are teasing me about my body (too skinny, too short, overweight, and so on).

G. Review

What did you learn about yourself and about other people in this step?

_____

_____

What did you learn from this step that made you feel better about yourself?

_____

_____

Now, add a statement to your barometer at the end of step 10.

Once you have completed the reading and exercises for this step, both you and an adult adviser should sign below. By doing so, you are solidifying your commitment to growing stronger and safer.

Adult Adviser's Signature _____

Reader's Signature _____

Even though it could feel right, it could be so wrong.

—Christian, aged sixteen

Evaluate Your Relationships and Activities

	Productive	or	Unproductive
My Activities List			
Am I spending my time in productive ways so I can reach my goal of becoming a street-safe person? Or am I wasting my time in unproductive activities?	Example: volunteering, teaching sports		Too much TV
	Assisting my teacher		Smoking

My Friends

Are my friends
pulling me up, or am
I letting them pull
me down? Are they
helping me discover
strength regardless of
painful situations? Or
are they feeding my
weaknesses?

Example: John Greenly
Name: _____

_____
Good leader, popular

Name: _____ Sammy Morris

_____
Cuts class, blames others

Name: _____

_____

Name: _____

Use the back of the page if you need
more space. _____

Step 2: Exercise B

Step 3

Handle Anger in a Positive Way

The third step in self-awareness—handle anger in a positive way—is simple to say, but it's not always so easy to do. If you practice self-discipline, however, you will soon learn that true power comes from within. In doing so, you will gradually make the maturity flip, as discussed in step 2. As you learn about—and practice—handling your anger responsibly, you can gain self-control.

One positive reward of learning to handle anger is that you will not inflict your feelings on others by lashing out with violent words or actions. At the same time, you will also be rewarded because you can learn how to respond and protect yourself when someone else is angry in your presence. Either way, you will be safer, whether you're on the street, at school, or in your home.

Anger grows when we feel we lack the power to control what is happening to us. As frustration builds, we may try to relieve negative emotions by escaping from reality. We may escape by drinking alcohol or taking drugs; just remember, escapes can turn into addictions. Or we may try to relieve the anger and frustration through violence. You can end up on either of these negative paths if you don't understand a basic spiritual principle. Just remember, we can't control other people; we can only control ourselves. For example, if I try to pick a fight with you and you walk away, you are in control. If I try to pick a fight with you and you fight back, I am in control because I got you to react to my anger and my bad behavior. As this example shows, learning to handle anger in a positive way is key to developing the self-control that is necessary to become a mature, empowered person.

A. Reverse Revenge

If someone hurts you or if you feel you have been wronged, there is an overwhelming temptation to right the wrong and strike back. You may satisfy your ego for the moment, but you can lose more than you gain. There is a big difference between using an incident as a learning experience and using it to take revenge. Before you react in anger, think it through. It is always a good idea to *sleep on it* before you do something you may regret. You have the inner power to reverse revenge and turn your life in a positive direction, if you will only choose to do so.

A Life Experience

In a courtroom case, a convicted child molester sexually abused Mary's son. She was so outraged that she shot the accused man to death in the courtroom and went to jail for it. Her young son needed his mother home to offer guidance so he could heal from the abuse he suffered. Mary's vengeance was self-destructive not only to herself but also to her family.

Questions to Consider

Mary was angry, which was okay, but her actions were not okay. What will you do if somebody hurts you this deeply? How can you turn a bad situation around and use it to help you grow stronger?

The following tips and ideas will give you practical tools for handling anger in a positive way and for stopping the cycle of revenge before it ruins your life:

- Don't jump to conclusions if you hear something that upsets you. If you don't know the facts firsthand, check them out. Someone could be spreading lies.
- If you plan to speak your mind, wait until you are calm, cool, and collected. A hot temper is nothing more than your ego defending itself. You can't be effective in anything you do if you can't control your behavior.
- When addressing a problem, don't use putdowns or insults. And don't bring up old issues. Stick to the problem at hand, and try to solve it.
- Don't spread rumors or gossip about others. It can come back to haunt you.
- Don't punish yourself for something someone else did. You are responsible for your behavior only. Remember, you can't change the behavior of others.
- Don't let anger fester. Forgive others, not for their sake, but for your own. When you do not forgive, you can become resentful, angry, and negative toward others. You can eventually lose your friends and self-esteem and become bitter about life.

Learn to laugh at yourself.

B. Use These Tips for Staying Cool

When you feel anger rising within you, the last thing you may want to do is to remain cool. You may feel you have no control over your anger. The truth is, anger is an emotion, and you can learn to manage it. It takes practice, but it can be done. Learn to handle anger at a young age so you won't make self-destructive decisions later.

Here are some tips for staying cool that may help you:

- If someone won't listen to your side of the story, speak up without raising your voice or being verbally abusive. Be politely persistent. Practice patience. It takes time to resolve problems.
- Conflict in the family is a breakdown in relationships. You can't fix anyone else. But if you focus on your own behavior and handle your anger responsibly, you will have a better chance of resolving family problems. Remember, everyone is special, and family members are also on their own journey of self-discovery.
- Develop an ability to *listen* without interrupting others!
- Silence is a powerful tool. Learn to use self-control. Pay attention, and notice when it is the right time to speak up and when you should be quiet. Talking too much can make a bad situation worse.
- Note—silence can be golden, but if you are experiencing neglect or mental or physical abuse, don't suffer in silence. Talk to someone outside your peer group. Get help from an adult you trust, a religious adviser, a school nurse, a school counselor, or a neighbor.
- Practice controlling your anger and standing up for yourself in a positive way, and it will become easier. Other people will begin to listen and learn from you.

A Life Experience

Anger blocks learning. Twenty high school students volunteered to help two low-income families fix up their homes. The adult leader divided the group into ten students per house to repair fences and paint walls. It was up to the students to pick a leader and delegate jobs. The first leader got angry when he felt his team was goofing off. He got frustrated and yelled at the group. He threw down his tools and stormed off, saying, "I quit." The second leader rotated assignments, gave the students frequent breaks, and set an example by working hard with a happy attitude.

Questions to Consider

In the preceding story, who felt a sense of accomplishment and had a rewarding experience? Have you ever been in a situation like this one? What did you do?

C. Let Go of Anger

Giving up anger and resentment toward others is a personal challenge. Too many people try to accomplish a goal without addressing issues that hold them back from making progress. Anger can be a *huge* stumbling block to your growth and maturity.

It preoccupies your mind, consumes your energy, and prevents you from solving problems. If you don't address your anger, it can take over your life. Giving in to your emotions does not always get you what you want.

A Life Experience

When Maria was in a private boarding school, a classmate asked if she could wear a gold pin that she had won in an art contest. Maria said absolutely not. Her classmate was offended and said she should have won the prize instead of Maria. A few days later, the pin was missing from Maria's dresser drawer. She told her roommates, and they searched her belongings. She retaliated by lying and accusing Maria of stealing her mother's ring. Maria found herself in the principal's office, trying to explain that her pin was missing—not the ring. Her classmate was cool under fire and convincing in her argument. Maria burst into tears of frustration. The principal believed that Maria must have stolen the ring and told Maria she would lose her privileges for three weeks or until she returned the ring. Maria received knowing smirks from her classmate as she headed to the study hall. Maria never saw her gold pin again. Although the experience was traumatic, Maria didn't hold on to her anger and resentment. Instead, she learned to be more understanding if someone asked for a favor. Maria also learned to stay cool when she felt angry and to present a stronger defense.

Questions to Consider

What would you feel if this happened to you? Would you have searched Tina's things? What other choices would you have?

The challenge of letting go of your anger can be particularly difficult when it comes to parents or adult guardians, but it is a crucial challenge that you must overcome regardless of how you feel. Do not hate or hold resentments toward your mother or father. All children have a strong spiritual bond with both parents regardless of how their parents behave. Anger can keep you from progressing and finding your own identity. Give up resentment, and you can become a stronger person.

A Life Experience

Nicole met a well-balanced and centered college freshman whose mother had died several years earlier. His father remarried and told him to leave their home because he had a new wife and two young boys to raise. At age eighteen, he reluctantly moved out and joined the air force. It took several years for him to resolve his anger and see the benefits of being on his own. It was a difficult learning experience, but when Nicole met this college freshman, he was wise beyond his years. He set an example for Nicole as he showed her how to give up her negative feelings toward her parents, who had drug abuse problems. Nicole began to see her parents as immature, troubled people with problems of their own. Eventually, Nicole realized that her parents' problems were not her fault.

D. Exercise Your Self-Awareness

These exercises in self-awareness will help you pinpoint your anger patterns and give you practical methods for changing those patterns. Working through these exercises will help you make the maturity flip so that you can grow stronger and empowered.

Exercise A: Analyze Your Anger

During the next week, make a note of each time you get angry. Try to think about anger as a learning experience and a time to develop patience with yourself and others. See if you can put yourself in the other person's shoes. Conflict is a critical part of learning how to handle your life. If you handle conflict in a mature way, it can teach you to grow in wisdom and self-awareness. After each incident, write out the answers to these questions in your notebook:

- What did this experience teach me?
- Could I have seen this problem coming?
- What can I do differently so I don't respond angrily to this situation again?

Exercise B: Inventory Your Relationships

First, write down in your notebook the name of one person who has caused you pain. How did you handle your relationship with this person? Does it still upset you? Was the issue resolved? If you see that person today, how will you feel about him or her? Did you deal with the conflict in a positive way?

Once you have looked at those who have caused you pain, flip the coin over and look at yourself. Use your notebook to make a list of people whose feelings you have hurt. Be honest with yourself. Everyone says something he or she doesn't mean or does something he or she regrets. Don't ignore problems—deal with them. To let go of bad feelings and to clear your conscience, you must acknowledge the pain you cause others. It takes courage to admit to being wrong, but you are building a stronger personality. And being courageous in this way can make you feel good about yourself. Most of the time, the other person will appreciate your honesty and forgive you. An apology can even make your relationship better.

After you offer an honest apology, it will be up to the other person to forgive you. That forgiveness may or may not come, but you have lifted the burden off your shoulders and learned from the experience. Who is on your list? Do you need to apologize to a friend or a member of your family? Are you willing to let go of the feeling that you were right and the other person was wrong?

Exercise C: Reduce Stress to Reduce Anger

You can reduce stress and develop a more positive outlook on life by improving your ability to stay calm. You can achieve this calm state anywhere and at any time by taking slow, deep breaths; closing your eyes; and counting to ten. You may also consider practicing meditation regularly to calm your mind. Meditation not only relaxes you, but when you get good at it, you can also discover new insights and solutions to problems. Try this simple exercise:

Relax—take deep breaths.

Pick a comfortable chair, close your eyes, and practice *not* thinking. If you like, play soft music. This exercise sounds easy, but you'll probably discover that all kinds of thoughts come popping up. If you get distracted, try again and see how long you can keep your mind free from any thoughts. You will soon see that your mind has flashbacks of events and people.

Take control of your thoughts.

We need to take control of and turn off all thoughts, especially negative ones. If you have experienced negative input from adults, you may need to reprogram your thoughts to be positive. Ask your higher power to help you. Repeat, "I am special," over and over, or focus on images from nature or beautiful art. The idea is to create a calm and quiet mind so you can grow stronger inwardly.

Relax your whole body.

Take a deep breath, and relax your toes, one at a time. Then slowly move up through your body and relax your legs, fingers, hands, and shoulders. Keep going up until you reach the top of your head, continuing to breathe slowly.

Practice this exercise twice a day.

Try to do this relaxation exercise for five minutes twice a day at first, and then gradually build up to twenty minutes per session or longer. With practice, you will be able to release the tension in your body and change your mind-set to a positive one. This exercise can teach you to stay calm so you can think and react better under the pressure of exams, social events, conflicts, or emergencies. You can build your self-awareness as you improve your ability to stay calm, cool, and collected.

E. Review

What did you learn about yourself and about other people in this step?

_____

_____

What did you learn from this step that made you feel better about yourself?

_____

_____

Now, add a statement to your barometer at the end of step 10.

Once you have completed the reading and exercises for this step, both you and an adult adviser should sign below. By doing so, you are solidifying your commitment to growing stronger and safer.

Adult Adviser's Signature _____

Reader's Signature _____

> Thinking about all the bad things in life makes
> it harder to experience the good.
>
> —Ali, aged eighteen

Step 4

Find Your Center

If someone puts a truck tire on one side of a car and a small spare tire on the other side, the car will be lopsided. Anyone riding in that car will be in for a bumpy ride. To work properly, the tires need to be equally balanced and aligned so the car can be centered and driven.

The same thing is true of us as human beings. When we feel inadequate, abused, angry, or intimidated, we get lopsided. When we are off-center, we are vulnerable, which means we're not safe. Vulnerability can make it easier for others to take advantage of us or to cause us harm. Or we may try to cover up that vulnerability by becoming the aggressor and hurting others.

As you can see, finding your center is a crucial step to becoming

Finding your center is life's challenge.

self-aware and street safe. But where is your center located? That is the challenge you face in step 4.

When you're centered, you are in a strong position to defend yourself, if necessary. Or you may be centered enough to avoid dangerous and abusive situations altogether. But when you're not centered, you're in a position of weakness where you can easily become a victim—or the flip side of a victim, which is a bully.

A. Define Your Center

Some people describe being centered in terms of feelings. When you are centered, you feel peaceful inside—not necessarily happy and peppy but calm and balanced. You're aware of problems, but they don't completely upset you. Being off-center may make you feel anxious, angry, or just sort of out of it. You don't feel like yourself on those days. On a deeper level, your center can be thought of as your heart and your conscience. It's an inner knowing that tells you the difference between right and wrong. It also tells you when you're headed toward danger or away from your true self. Sometimes, you'll hear people say things like "In my heart, I knew he was lying, but I wanted to believe him" or "Something inside me knew better." That *something* is your intuitive center.

B. Avoid the Downward Spiral of Negativity

Human beings are separated from animals because we are given a freedom of choice and a conscience to protect us and to help us make good decisions. If you are off-center, you may have a negative attitude that says, "I get what I want no matter whom I hurt." You may try to justify your actions—gossiping, cheating, lying, stealing, or abusing others—but you will be caught by your own conscience, and your behavior can eventually take a toll on your mental, physical, and spiritual health.

The first time a young person goes against his or her conscience is the hardest. The next time, it gets a little easier, and so on. Little by little, the conscience shuts down so you don't feel the pain of bad choices. A girl may be nervous the first time she shoplifts. She knows in her heart it is wrong, but she is an egocentric, "I want" person. The next time, it's a little easier as the off-center ego grows, and she begins to believe she won't get caught. Suppose a young boy decides to steal something from his neighbor's garage. He too is off-center and may graduate to purse snatching or burglary. Or he may join a gang where he has to prove himself by beating up another teen.

Criminal behavior is a self-destructive downward spiral. When you decide to go against your conscience, you have not made the maturity flip. You are thinking only of the immediate gratification for "I need" and "I want," with little thought to future consequences. In the early stage of becoming a violent person, the individual may feel immediate remorse. Gradually, however, he or she forgets this remorse and escalates his or her violent behavior. (See more on this pattern in the section on "Stages in the Cycle of Abuse" in part D of step 6.) The out-of-control bully is consumed by anger and strikes out abusively at others. He or she shuts down his or her conscience and probably shows no remorse for misdeeds.

All these ego-centered, off-balanced individuals may not know how to change their behavior, but people do have the power to change their behaviors from negative toward the positive. Finding your center and staying centered is life's challenge. It can be done if you face up to the pain you cause. Ask your higher power to help you become more self-aware. The sooner you get your life centered, the sooner you can start reaching for your unlimited potential.

As you make a spiritual journey, you are either moving up and becoming self-aware, or you're on a downward spiral leading to isolation and despair. The question for each one of us is, "Do I love myself enough to grow strong from within and become centered?" But if you don't become centered, the question is, "How much pain do I want in my life?"

C. Find Your Center between Being a Bully and a Pincushion

Your goal is to become centered so you can find your true identity. There is a big difference between being overly sensitive and being overly assertive. In order to live a healthy, happy, and productive life, you must search for your center. That center falls between the two extremes of being a bully on one side and a person with pincushion sensitivity on the other, as you'll see in the discussion that follows.

1. Pincushion People

If you are quiet and overly sensitive, you are focusing too much time and energy on yourself and your needs. You can become like a *pincushion*— one who cries out anytime someone or something pricks your surface. Instead of being self-centered, direct your attention to making

Open up and reach out.

others feel comfortable. Grow stronger by thinking about how you can help someone else. Get involved in positive activities. Explore your potential by offering to become a volunteer. Practice speaking up in class and express your ideas to friends. Do not be overly concerned with other people's opinions. Do what you think is right within your heart. Find a specific interest, such as art, science, music, the environment, or sports. Get involved in helping others! You need to develop your own identity. If you do for others, you can grow in self-confidence.

The overly sensitive, or pincushion, person must learn to walk away from a bully. No one should tolerate being treated as a victim. If you encounter controlling behavior, see it as a challenge and a test of your self-awareness.

2. Being a Bully

The bully tries to boss others and may use intimidation to get his or her way. The bully must learn to modify his or her behavior. A bully can become a strong leader if he or she learns to channel his or her negative, controlling behavior into a more positive approach to life. Both girls and boys can be bullies. Girls often fall into the victim category and boys the bully, but that's not always the case.

If you know you have a tendency to bully others, practice self-control; count to ten, walk away, and learn to laugh at yourself. Stay away from people who upset you until you get a handle on your emotions.

Ask family members and friends to help you by respectfully calling attention to your behavior. Get involved in team activities so you can learn the value of cooperation and teamwork. Listen to others, and don't be defensive! Be patient. Your goal is to turn negative behavior around and become centered so you can build good relationships. If your anger is out of control, seek help immediately.

3. Become Centered on Safety

One trait that both pincushion types and bullies have in common is that they are reactors. They allow outside influences and other people to shape their thoughts and actions. The bully reacts by hurting others, and the pincushion people react by hurting themselves, but both are driven by outer events. By contrast, someone who is centered is not compelled to react to what others do and say. Centered people draw on a strong, spiritual inner core to guide them toward good choices. They are driven by their own values and convictions, not by the whims of others. The following descriptions will help you get a better picture of all three types of people. Perhaps you see a little of all three types in yourself or your friends. Take a critical look at yourself to find your center.

Pincushion People	Bully
needy, dependent	aggressive, confrontational
shy, quiet	angry, abusive
easily intimidated; feels isolated, alone	tries to control people and events
possible victim of abuse	likes to boss others
suffers in silence	blames or victimizes others
takes out pain on self through drugs, mutilation, and so on	demeans others
gang follower	abuses others physically, sexually, or mentally
feels like a victim; too sensitive, emotional	inflated ego, controller
thinks about suicide	misuses power

Centered

listens to others with an open mind
maintains strong personal values about right and wrong
tries not to judge; forgives others
exhibits patience; can negotiate an agreement
manages personal emotions and cares about others' feelings
treats him- or herself and others with respect
speaks up without anger; doesn't harbor resentments
apologizes for mistakes
works to develop self-awareness, self-confidence, self-discipline, and self-control

A Life Experience

Tia and her family moved back to California after living in the Hawaiian Islands. Tia and her grandmother were driving to the store one day when her grandmother asked her what the most important thing she learned in Hawaii was. Tia thought about it for a few minutes and said, "I learned how to be popular from a new girl at my old school." Her grandmother was surprised by her answer and asked what she meant. "Well," Tia said, "Jessica arrived mid-semester, and it wasn't long before she was the most popular girl in school. I couldn't figure it out at first, until I noticed she was friendly, interested in others, always had a smile, didn't gossip, and treated everyone with respect. She was such an upbeat person she made you feel good. I decided to try it when I moved here. It sure helped me get off on the right foot at my new school."

SPIRITUALLY CENTERED AND SAFE

Centered people are less likely to be victims because they have the self-esteem and self-awareness to demonstrate respect for themselves and others. They draw on their inner core of strength to guide their choices in life.

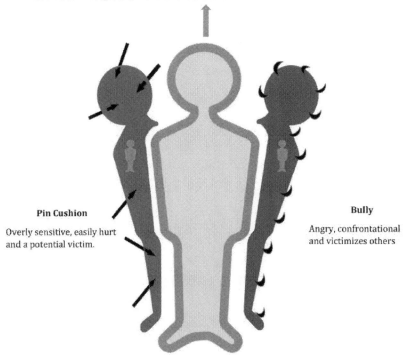

Pin Cushion

Overly sensitive, easily hurt and a potential victim.

Bully

Angry, confrontational and victimizes others

©SafeKidsNow.com

Questions to Consider

Tia was describing a centered young person. How do you let people know they are special and deserve respect? How do you show an interest in others? What do you need to work on to become more centered?

D. Avoid Off-Center People

The bully and the pincushion person are the opposite ends of the spectrum. The bully looks for the pincushion type to make him or her cry, get upset, or show fear. That makes the bully feel powerful. These off-center individuals are filling a void in one another. A bully boyfriend needs a pincushion girlfriend who will tolerate his controlling behavior. A bully father needs an intimidated mother. A gang leader needs pincushion followers. A cult leader needs lost, hurting souls so he can control their lives. A dictator needs a nation of followers.

Beware! Don't put other people on a pedestal or treat them as if they have more talent, wisdom, and knowledge than anyone else. You may be diminishing yourself and others. We are all imperfect.

Abuse of power has been going on for centuries. When citizens are spiritually off-center, the culture is divided into leaders and followers. Perceived power in leaders is seductive to followers because they don't understand their own inner strength and often feel that they don't have any power of their own. So-called leaders can abuse power and divide the culture into cults, hate groups, militias, and gangs. These spiritually off-center individuals can make our streets and our homes dangerous for everyone.

If someone wants to control what you do and whom you can see, run the other way. These individuals or groups may look like friends and promise happiness, but don't be fooled. They only want power and control over you.

A Life Experience

Jim Jones was a respected minister in San Francisco before he led hundreds of his followers to Guyana in the late 1970s. When the cult was criticized for abusing its followers, a US congressman flew to Guyana to investigate. After being exposed for abuses, Jim Jones ordered the congressman killed and his followers to commit mass suicide. Nine hundred men, women, and children followed Jim Jones into death. (Religious cults control people's behavior. Responsible religions empower people.)

For more information,

http://www.biography.com/people/jim-jones-10367607.

Questions to Consider

Can you think of any other examples of people abusing their power to control others in America or elsewhere in the world?

E. Exercise Your Self-Awareness

These exercises will give you an opportunity to find and strengthen your center, which will help you immensely as you continue to grow and mature.

Exercise A: Learn from Others

Everyone you meet can teach you lessons about yourself. With a little practice, you can tell if you are interacting with a pincushion, bully, or spiritually centered person, or a combination of all three. Self-awareness can give you the power to see the stage of personal growth that others have reached. Use the worksheet at the end of this step to make a list of friends, classmates, relatives, and neighbors. Try to figure out if they are pincushions, bullies, or centered people. What can you learn from each of these people?

Exercise B: Identify Your Strengths and Weaknesses

You cannot focus on strengthening a weakness until you identify what you need to work on. Make two columns in your notebook. On one side, list strengths. On the other side, list weaknesses. The following examples contain ideas to get you started.

Strengths	**Weaknesses**
(Examples)	(Examples)
Artistic, creative	Poor writer
Athletic	Lacks confidence, insecure
Persistent	Quiet, shy
Patient	Has trouble expressing self
Good listener	Slow reader

Once you complete your list, be creative in looking for ways to improve and challenge yourself to go beyond your previous limits. Start where you are slightly uncomfortable. That means push yourself into doing something you are afraid to do. Take small steps to build your confidence. For example, if you have trouble expressing yourself, try to speak up more in class or get acquainted with a classmate you don't know well and show an interest by asking questions and listening. If you are scared to read in front of people, read out loud to younger children in the neighborhood or at school. Get to know your neighbors and offer to help them with small projects. Or try some of these ideas: Volunteer to help at a church, community, or youth center. Strengthen your writing skills by joining a writing club, working on the school yearbook, reporting for the school newspaper, or composing letters to the editor.

To develop positive-thinking skills, all you need is a desire to improve yourself. By tapping into your strengths and improving your weak areas, you can develop self-esteem and find your real center.

Exercise C: Track Your Time

Keep a log. Each day for a week, write down what you do and how much time you spend doing each activity. This exercise can help you organize and balance your time to be more productive. Being balanced helps you stay centered. Make a pie chart to show the amount of time you spend at each activity.

The list at the end of this exercise covers a number of areas where you may spend time. Use it or add your own descriptions to show where your time goes. At the end of the week, assign a percentage value to each activity and transfer that information to a pie chart. (See the "Track Your Time" chart at the end of this step.)

Your goal is to become aware of where your day goes. Do you need to spend more time with your family or on your schoolwork? Focus more on building relationships or changing your attitude than on time-wasting activities. Date and post your pie chart. Make a new pie chart in six months, and compare it with the old one. Keep your evaluations for future reference. Make a commitment to turn unproductive time into productive time for yourself.

There is nothing as fulfilling as seeing progress based on your own initiative. You can boost your self-esteem as you transform yourself into a centered, confident person. Becoming self-motivated gets easier as you see progress. The more you do to improve your life, the greater the reward.

Here is a list of activities you may wish to include in your pie chart:

School	(hours including studying)
Work	(home chores, after-school work)
Family	(doing things together)
Physical activity	(exercising, working out)
Spiritual reflection	(self-awareness/improvement)
Recreation	(movies, TV, and so on)
Hobby, computer	(doing something you like to do)
Community involvement	(doing for others, self-development)
Developing relationships	(parties, hanging around, loafing)
Other	(activities not listed)

F. Review

What did you learn about yourself and about other people in this step?

_____

_____

What did you learn from this step that made you feel better about yourself?

_____

_____

Now, add a statement to your barometer at the end of step 10.

Once you have completed the reading and exercises for this step, both you and an adult adviser should sign below. By doing so, you are solidifying your commitment to growing stronger and safer.

Adult Adviser's Signature _____

Reader's Signature _____

> You make more friends in two months by becoming
> interested in other people than you can in two years
> by trying to get others interested in you.
>
> —Dale Carnegie

Track Your Time

Sample Pie Chart

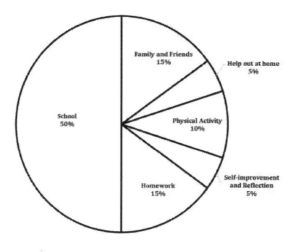

Create your own pie chart to track your time.

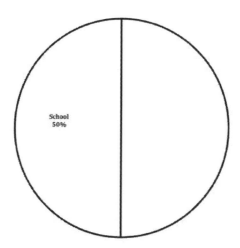

Exercise C

Learn from Others

	Pincushion		Spiritually Centered		Bully
Example:					
	Maria Salvio		*Anita Martinez*		*Mason Emerson*
	Shy, timid		Forgiving, patient		Bossy, angry, vengeful
	Amy Smith		*Anselmo Stuart*		*Mr. Williams*
	Quiet, alone		Helpful, listens, respects others		Mean to kids
1.		1.		1.	
2.		2.		2.	
3.		3.		3.	
4.		4.		4.	
5.		5.		5.	
6.		6.		6.	

7.		7.			7.	
8.		8.			8.	

Exercise A

Step 5

Trust Your Intuition and Instincts

Centered individuals trust their instincts for self-protection. As we grow in maturity and nurture ourselves spiritually, our intuition grows stronger. Learning to trust your intuition and instincts—the challenge of step 5—is an important part of becoming empowered and street safe. All living creatures receive warning signs of impending danger through their instincts and intuition. But we have to be self-aware in order to recognize them. If the actions of others or your surroundings don't feel right or you feel apprehensive, trust your intuition and react immediately. Stay alert. You have good instincts. Pay attention.

A. Understand Your Instincts

What exactly is an *instinct*? What about *intuition*? To begin to answer those questions, here are the Merriam-Webster Dictionary definitions for these words:

Instincts can protect you.

Instinct—"a natural impulse; behavior that is below the conscious level"

Intuition—"the power to direct knowledge without rational thought; quick and ready insight"

It's common to wonder where these insights come from. You will have to decide for yourself what you believe about this issue. Many people believe that intuition and instincts are the Creator's way of protecting us and that each one of us has a guardian angel. But we have to acknowledge and welcome this protection and look for this help. Marcella calls her guardian angel Saint Catherine. Jacob calls his angel White Oak, who was a wise old Native American chief. Whenever Jacob has a big problem—or even a small one—he calls on White Oak for help, whether he needs a parking place or the wisdom to handle an alcoholic relative.

While Marcella and Jacob depend on their angels, other people may believe in calling out directly to God or to the Holy Spirit or to the name of a deity in their own religious tradition. As stated already, you will have to make your own personal decision about this issue, but you should know that a higher power is always there in one form or another to protect and guide you. You only have to ask for help and listen, which will take practice.

The following examples, based on true stories, can help you get a better picture of how your instincts and intuition can protect you.

A Life Experience

Dan arrived home after school and walked up to his front door as he usually did. But when he went past the large picture window, he felt instinctively that something was wrong. He hesitated at the door with the key in his hand. Instead of walking in, he decided to ring his own doorbell. He heard footsteps inside the house, but he knew his family was not home. He walked calmly over to his neighbor's house and called the police. Two men who were burglarizing Dan's house were caught climbing over the back fence.

A Life Experience

Kim, aged twelve, was walking home from school one day. When a car slowly passed her, Kim became suspicious as her intuition kicked in. She started walking faster as the car stopped in front of her. A man walked around the car and opened the passenger door just as Kim passed by. He grabbed her by the backpack, shoved her toward the car, and ordered her to get in. Kim stayed calm, slipped out of the shoulder harness, and ran away, leaving the man holding her backpack. He slammed the pack to the ground and drove off.

Questions to Consider

Can you think of any times when you noticed your instincts or intuition at work? Have you ever had an experience in which your intuition protected you?

B. Pay Attention to Your Intuition

You may take your intuition for granted, or you may not even realize that you are capable of unique insights. To develop your intuition, you need to pay attention to what goes on around you. Look around, and notice who is at the park or in the mall. Scan the street when you're walking on the sidewalk. Does everything feel okay? When people have taken action based on their intuition, it has saved lives. One family decided to postpone a trip and missed being in the middle of a major car wreck. Another person felt she should call a friend whom she hadn't talked to in a year. She discovered her friend was desperately ill and had been trying to contact her. A couple became restless and felt they needed to go home early from a party. They arrived in time to see burglars trying to break into their house.

By contrast, many people are *not* in touch with their intuition. It's not uncommon for a crime victim to say, "I knew I shouldn't have let that man in my house, but I was too embarrassed to have him wait on the doorstep," or "I had a bad feeling the minute I stepped into the elevator alone with that person," or "I know I should have asked my friend to walk me to my car." If these victims had relied on their instincts, they might have stayed safe.

A Life Experience

James was in an unfamiliar neighborhood to visit an old friend. As he got off the bus, he didn't feel comfortable about his surroundings. He went to a gas station and called his friend to pick him up instead of walking down the dark blocks alone.

A Life Experience

Mary was walking down the street. She felt she was being followed. She crossed the street, and a man behind her crossed the street too. Mary could feel he was getting closer. She turned around and got a good look at him. That surprised him as she walked back across the street into a well-lit drugstore. The man disappeared around the corner as Mary called the police, who came to her assistance and drove her home.

A Life Experience

Gina always walked home from school with two friends. But one afternoon, one friend was sick and the other had to stay after school. They usually took a shortcut through the park, which was in an isolated area. Gina could have gone that way, but instead, she decided to take the long route and stay on the main street.

Questions to Consider

Have you ever changed your plans because you had a *bad feeling* about something? Have you ever gone ahead into a situation even though you felt uneasy about it and then regretted your decision?

C. Unblock Your Intuition: Avoid Self-Destructive Secrets

Just as you need to rely on your intuition for guidance and protection, you must also protect yourself by refusing to keep self-destructive secrets. A negative secret can involve drugs, sexual abuse, molestation, violence, or something you are embarrassed to tell. It can become like a wound that will not heal, because you can't keep a negative secret from your conscience. If you are centered, your instincts will tell you to be honest with yourself and others. You may try to push the secret away from the surface, but it keeps popping up in your head even if you try to ignore it. If something bad happens to you, it's crucial for you to tell a trusted adult. It's easier to solve problems as soon as they occur. Don't wait for the problem to grow—find help. Don't let the negative secret take over your life. If ignored, your grades, relationships, and health, both mental and physical, can suffer.

A Life Experience

When David was young, his father's drinking problem made it impossible to invite friends home. One afternoon, David found his dad drunk and talking strangely about wanting to die. As he consoled him, the doorbell rang. David's friends wanted to know why he was taking so long to come out because they were going skateboarding. He was trying to think up an excuse when his dad hollered, "Tell them to come on in if they want to see a no-good drunk." David's heart sank as he realized the family secret was no longer a secret. The boys quickly turned away, saying, "See you later," and whispering to each other as they disappeared down the street.

Questions to Consider

If you learned about a self-destructive secret, what would you do? Do you think it would bother your conscience if you ignored this secret plea for help? Would you tell a parent, teacher, counselor, or another trusted adult? Or would you gossip and spread rumors as David feared his friends would do?

Sometimes, so many lies can build up that you create an entirely separate, secret life. If you lie to cover up a secret life, you are weaving a self-destructive web. You can lie to others and think you are getting away with it, but your conscience knows the truth and you are going directly against your better, self-protective instincts. To avoid having a painful conscience, you may try to ignore what it's telling you. Gradually disconnecting from your conscience allows you to compartmentalize your feelings, but eventually, you'll pay a high price in terms of your mental, spiritual, and physical health.

A secret life built on finding pleasure and escaping reality can take over everything you do. That is called an

Be honest with yourself and others.

addiction. It slowly takes over the real you. If you shoplift and lie about drugs, admit the problem to yourself. If you can't tell the truth about what you do, you are setting yourself up for pain and suffering. You are growing from the ego side of yourself, not the spiritual side, and your lies can eventually destroy your character, your reputation, and your instincts.

A Life Experience

A radio talk show host was discussing secret lives. A man called in to say he was a good father, a loving husband, and an executive with a large company. His secret was he used pornography and that led him into degrading and dangerous situations. His fantasy had turned into an obsession that was destroying him. His time, energy, and money went into his obsession or into covering it up. He could no longer control his behavior. He planned to kill himself so he wouldn't disgrace his family.

Questions to Consider

Can you name any famous celebrities who had secret lives of drug abuse, sexual misconduct, or violent behavior? Some names from the past might include Elvis Presley, Marilyn Monroe, Janis Joplin, and River Phoenix. Can you name famous people today who had secret lives that eventually caught up to them?

D. Exercise Your Self-Awareness

Your instincts and intuition are key components of self-awareness. Use these exercises to identify the damaging effects of negative secrets and the positive impact of trusting your own special insights.

Exercise A: Uncover Self-Destructive Secrets

Drug use is the most common type of secret life for young people, and it can lead you into dangerous situations where you ignore the warnings of your instincts and intuition. In the following section, you will see some clues to help you decide if your behavior is becoming self-destructive. Drug addiction is a progressive disease, and changes in your life can be so gradual you may not recognize what's happening. So be honest. Do you see this behavior in yourself or your friends? Write down your answers to these statements in your notebook:

- I feel comfortable with friends who use drugs.
- I try drugs occasionally.
- I am becoming moody, angry, hostile, short-tempered, and defiant to authority at school or at home, and there's a change in my sleeping patterns.

- My grades are going down, but I don't care.
- I have less motivation, but I tell myself I can handle it.
- I am more isolated at school.
- My social group is getting smaller.

By facing these issues, you have taken an important step in breaking the hold of drug addiction—or some other type of secret life—for yourself or someone close to you. Only you can make the choice to wake up and change what's going on. Once you make that decision, all types of resources are available to you. Get help from a hotline, counseling program, or twelve-step group. Talk to a parent, minister, rabbi, or some other religious adviser. Find a trusted adult who can point you in the right direction—you're worth it! (Use the "Step 5: Exercise A" chart at the end of this chapter to plot your progress in breaking the hold of a secret life.)

Exercise B: Test Your Instincts

Your instincts are integral to your being a centered person. Your safety may depend on how well you pay attention and rely on those instincts. How safe are you? Circle the number that best describes your opinion, with 1 indicating strong disagreement and 5 indicating strong agreement.

	Disagree			Agree	
I know drugs and alcohol can reduce my self-awareness.	1	2	3	4	5
I will not drive with anyone who has been drinking.	1	2	3	4	5
I stay alert to my surroundings when I'm out at night.	1	2	3	4	5
I am less likely to be a victim because I listen to my instincts.	1	2	3	4	5

If someone gets angry, I don't react. I can walk away.	1	2	3	4	5
If a stranger tries to separate me from friends at a party, I won't go.	1	2	3	4	5
If I feel uncomfortable about doing something, I don't do it.	1	2	3	4	5
If I'm uneasy at a party, I can ask a friend to take me home.	1	2	3	4	5
If a party gets out of control, I will leave.	1	2	3	4	5
I will call home if I need transportation.	1	2	3	4	5
If I don't feel safe about a shortcut, I will refuse to go.	1	2	3	4	5
I can stay calm and evaluate what to do in an emergency.	1	2	3	4	5
I practice staying calm so I won't panic in a crisis.	1	2	3	4	5
I practice using my instincts for self-protection.	1	2	3	4	5
I will not keep harmful secrets. I will find help to solve problems.	1	2	3	4	5

My total is

A low score is 15, and a high score is 75. If you are below 50, you need to work on trusting your instincts and acting on them.

E. Review

What did you learn about yourself and about other people in this step?

_____

_____

What did you learn from this step that made you feel better about yourself?

_____

_____

Now, add a statement to your barometer at the end of step 10.

Once you have completed the reading and exercises for this step, both you and an adult adviser should sign below. By doing so, you are solidifying your commitment to growing stronger and safer.

Adult Adviser's Signature _____

Reader's Signature _____

> All that we are is the result of what we have thought. The mind is everything. What we think, we become.
>
> —Buddha

A Secret Life Is Self-Destructive

Negative secrets, such as being molested, stealing, taking drugs, lying, misusing sex, and hurting others, will have consequences to my spirit and safety. I may look okay on the outside, but I am unhappy on the inside. I can grow stronger based on my choices today. Who will listen to me?

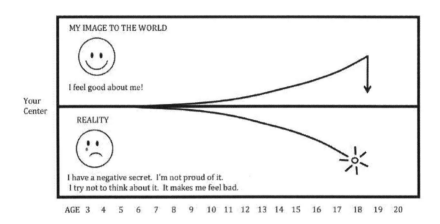

Do you have secrets that cause anxiety or depression?
Chart how you feel about yourself. What do you see?

Chart Your Feelings

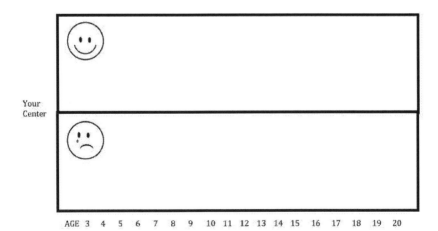

Step 6

Take Charge of Your Life

In step 1, we discussed how special you are as an individual. When you feel within yourself that you are worthy of love, then you will respect yourself and show respect to others. In step 2, we examined the fact that emotional and physical pain is part of life. You must learn to work with that pain to grow stronger. Step 3 helped you deal with anger and showed how you can speak up in a calm, assertive way. Step 4 focused on finding your center in order to build your self-awareness and self-esteem. Step 5 encouraged you to practice relying on your instincts to be safer and more confident. Now, step 6 can help you take charge of your life by knowing how to react to problems and problem people in a positive way, a skill that can keep you street safe wherever you are. Taking charge of your life means taking full responsibility for yourself because you have the power to meet any challenge, regardless of what has happened in the past.

A. Make a Choice to Take Charge

As you take charge of your life, you can master self-control skills. You may discover you are wiser than you think and that you can find solutions to problems that seem unsolvable. As you gain insights, you will discover bullies will not anger you. You will not tolerate an abusive relationship. You will not feel the need to take drugs, misuse sex, join a gang, or be dependent on others for your identity. You will have learned that life is hard enough without putting yourself in the position of solving more difficult problems. Learn these lessons early in life, and you can be successful beyond your wildest dreams.

Taking charge of your life essentially comes down to making a choice. You can choose to let circumstances and problems define you, or you can choose to rise above them. You can choose to stay on a self-destructive path, or you can change direction. Taking charge of your life doesn't mean you have to be arrogant or ego driven. Rather, it means you make wise choices that are consistent with your commitment to being a spiritually centered, street-safe person.

A Life Experience

Cathy was fifteen when her mother and her mother's boyfriend moved from New York to Mexico. She entered Mexico City College because there was no English-speaking high school near her new home. One day, her mother and the boyfriend told her she would stay in Mexico. They had to return to the United States on urgent business. Her mother told Cathy she would send her money, but the checks never arrived. Cathy had to figure out how to survive. She talked to the dean of women at her school and became an interpreter for tourists.

She gave up her regular classes to focus on improving her Spanish and learning Mexican history. A Spanish-speaking friend taught her how to bargain for vegetables at the market, and she used that skill to negotiate with cabdrivers and tourists. She was forced to come out of her shell and meet new people as she took visitors on sightseeing tours. Though that period of her life was difficult, Cathy learned she could survive as she discovered hidden talents. She could speak up, talk with adults as an equal, and make tough decisions. She grew in self-confidence and went from being an immature child to someone who could take charge of her life—all within a few short months.

Questions to Consider

What choices did Cathy make that showed she was taking charge of her life? What would have happened if she had made different choices? What would you have done if you had been in Cathy's situation?

B. Stand Your Ground

Taking charge of your life can make other people angry because they may find out they can't control your behavior. When it comes to making decisions that affect how you value yourself, you will need to be assertive.

Remember, you have to feel special within yourself. No one can do that for you. The way to feel special is to respect yourself and your body. Don't let anyone talk you into doing anything that will have consequences that go against your values and conscience. Stand up for yourself.

A Life Experience

Cathy was asked out on a double date in Mexico City. After a movie, the girls' dates, who were college-aged men, took them to a bar. The other couple and Cathy's date had too much to drink. Cathy was uncomfortable as she slowly sipped one beer. An hour later, the other couple disappeared upstairs. Cathy's date grabbed her hand and wanted her to follow. Cathy refused. He was extremely angry and made a scene. The men at the bar encouraged him to take control of Cathy. She stood up and told him if he didn't stop, she would report him to the university authorities. His attitude changed immediately, and they drove home in silence. Cathy didn't win any friends, but she gained valuable experience in learning to stand up for herself.

Questions to Consider

What could Cathy have done differently not to get into this situation in the first place? Why did her date act like that? What would you have done?

C. Let Logic Rule

Are you aware of how you make important decisions in your life? Do you base your decisions on logic or emotion? If you are emotionally involved in a situation, you may not see reality clearly. Your goal is to know yourself better. If you go against your Creator's laws, you need to ask yourself, "How much pain do I want in my life?" Before you make any life-changing choices, evaluate your decision-making process. Do your decisions help you take charge of your life or leave you in a more vulnerable position? For young people, there are two areas where they can easily be swayed by emotions or peer pressure: sex and drugs. In the sections that follow, we'll take a closer look at these two areas and see how you can learn to let logic rule.

1. Don't Sell Yourself Short

An important aspect of taking charge of your life is being responsible for your sexual activity. Magazines, books, movies, and television writers use sexually explicit stories because they sell. Sex is a strong human desire and not something to be treated lightly. Beware! Intimate sexual contact is a spiritual bonding with another human being. That bonding explains why some sexual partners may stay together in spite of violent or unfaithful behavior. This bond is a gift given to couples to help them stay together. Don't misuse it. Choose a centered lifetime partner by taking time to know that person's values, character, and commitment to you. You are worth it. Don't sell yourself short.

Now, consider this example in terms of basing decisions on logic or emotions:

> *Situation:* My boy- or girlfriend is pressuring me to have sex. What should I do?

> *My emotions say* I feel he or she will leave me if I don't say yes. I will do anything for him or her. The most important thing is being together. He or she makes me feel special, happy, and loved. I don't want to lose him or her.

> *Logic says* I don't want to risk getting a venereal disease, like AIDS, or becoming pregnant. A baby is a huge responsibility. How will I support a baby? Many couples break up after they have sex because they are not emotionally centered. I want to make sure I am mature and have my own identity before I become a mother or father. I'm not ready to make a lifelong commitment. I will no longer be a carefree teen enjoying my friends and parties. If we really love each other, we can wait.

A Life Experience

Jamie was engaged to a college student who was five years older and an ex-military man. They decided not to have sex because they wanted their relationship to be based on love and friendship. They were married one year later. During their forty years of marriage, they never worried about the other one cheating. They established a committed relationship *before* they got married.

A Life Experience

Marcia volunteered at a homeless shelter. One day, they were short of helpers. A young man stepped out of the line of people waiting for food and offered to help serve. He looked older than his thirty years with his hair slicked back in a ponytail and scars on his face. Marcia learned he was an ex-convict and a recovering heroin addict in a methadone treatment program. He was desperate to turn his life around so he would not go back to prison. Every Saturday, they talked. He didn't know how to deal with the pain of an abusive father who murdered his mother. He had a bad temper and used it to control his environment. His father abused women, so he had no idea how to respect women. In fact, his rage had led him to convictions for rape, assault, and attempted murder. He admitted he needed to practice self-control but did not know where to start. His biggest frustration was with women, and he once exclaimed, "They need knocking around sometimes."

After several discussions, Marcia suggested he stop playing the field and concentrate on getting his life together. Even after all he had been through, he just stared at Marcia when she suggested that he leave women alone for a while. "No way," he protested. "I love women!" Marcia realized she'd have to be creative to get through to him. So she tried broadening his horizons by explaining that some countries have laws to keep women from leaving their homes and that women have to cover themselves from head to foot so men can stay in control, but in a free society, there are no restrictions. Marcia went on to say, "In the United States, men glorify women. But some women have learned there is money and power in flirting, wearing provocative clothes, and making a man feel good to get what she wants." Then she added, "We even teach little girls how to be sexually attractive."

The young man thought about what Marcia had said, and the next week, he told her, "It sounds like men have created their own downfall." Once he made that realization, he started taking charge of his life. He began to get his life in order so women and drugs couldn't control him. He knew it would be a long journey because he would have to completely change his lifestyle. He was beginning to see he had the power to change instead of blocking his pain by using drugs. He acknowledged he had to take responsibility for his actions. He gradually gave up his anger and started setting goals. He attended church and found the support he needed to discover his own identity.

Questions to Consider

Do you think Jamie and her husband let logic rule in their relationship? What choices led Marcia's homeless man down his self-destructive path? What did he do to change direction? How did the people in both of these life-experience stories take charge of their lives?

2. Don't Give in to Peer Pressure

Unless preteens and teens are centered and spiritually strong, it's very easy for them to be influenced by their friends and peer group, especially when it comes to using drugs and alcohol. Everyone wants to be accepted by others, but if you try to gain that acceptance by going against your principles, then the person your friends accept is not really you. It's a false image of you. Besides, giving in to others is exactly the opposite of taking charge of your life. It's up to you to chart your course toward becoming a mature, responsible person, because you are the one who will live with the consequences if you don't.

Take a look at this example to see the interplay of logic and emotions in regard to drug and alcohol use.

> *Situation:* You feel pressure to drink and take drugs at parties. Why not join the crowd?

> *My emotions say* my friends love to party and have fun. I want to be included. Just one or two beers or a joint can't hurt. Everyone's doing it. We have such a good time, and it's harmless.

> *Logic says* this is risky behavior. Alcohol and drugs lower resistance and make people less aware of their surroundings. Drinking and drugs make people say and do stupid things. I need to be alert and in control of myself at all times so I won't be embarrassed or do something I will regret. I have to live with my conscience tomorrow.

A Life Experience

Trina started doing drugs when she was thirteen because she wanted to impress an older boy she liked. As drugs took over her life, she dropped out of school and ended up living on the streets. When she was homeless, she was raped. Trina traded sex for money and hit bottom the night she was almost killed by another drug addict who wanted her money. She found a church and asked her higher power for strength. She used that experience to take charge of her life and change herself. She stopped taking drugs, moved into an abandoned car, dressed at a shelter, and got a part-time job. She became self-sufficient, and her self-esteem grew. She found herself by reaching out to others and organizing a self-help group for homeless women. Eventually, Trina got a better place to live, a better job, and a better life.

Questions to Consider

What choices did Trina make that led her into homelessness? What could she have done differently? How did Trina turn her life around?

D. Choose Not to Be Abused

People who tolerate abuse are off-center and may make excuses for a gradual escalation of abuse. They are no longer in control of their lives. As the bully grows more controlling, the victim becomes more isolated and dependent. A relationship in which neither partner is centered can be turbulent. As the bully gets stronger, the victim gets weaker; he or she stops speaking up and becomes too embarrassed to tell others. Eventually, the abuse can become so bad that it leads to serious injury or even death.

Abuse doesn't just happen overnight. Generally, it takes place in three different stages, which are described here. Bullies can be boys or girls, men or women. The scenario here uses male pronouns. But remember, girls can also try to control boys.

Stages in the Cycle of Abuse

1. *The tension-building stage* is where you feel like you are walking on eggshells so you won't upset him or her.
2. *The controlling stage* is when he or she gets jealous, threatens you and others, or becomes violent.
3. *The hearts and flowers stage* is when he or she makes you feel special and promises never to do it again. If you believe him or her, you are caught in the cycle of abuse.

For someone in this situation, the voices of logic and emotion may sound like this:

Situation: I love my boyfriend, but he is jealous and has a bad temper. At first, he made me feel special, but now he wants to control my life. I am trying to get him to stop it.

My emotions say I care about my boyfriend. I know he can change. I can help him. I'll stick by him. He says he needs me and he will change.

Logic says be honest. He's not treating you with respect and love. He needs to seek counseling immediately. If he's going to change, he's got to show it. He's got to be the one to change, not me. If I stay with him, I'm going to get hurt—maybe even killed. (Note—the Johns Hopkins Bloomberg School of Public Health has reported that in a twenty-nation study, one in every three women are abused.)

Self-Awareness Alert

Run—don't walk—away if a boyfriend or girlfriend is abusively controlling your relationship. Over time, abusive behavior gets worse, not better. When people use their own wills to control others, they are not centered. Teenagers who are centered will not put up with abusive, controlling relationships. Remember, you can't change anyone else, but you can save yourself a lot of pain by developing your inner strength and self-awareness.

E. Exercise Your Self-Awareness

Have you taken charge—and taken responsibility—for your own life? When you face challenges and problems, do you rise to the occasion, or do you fall back into the childish position of a victim? The exercises for this step will help you identify areas where you have been successful and those where you need work to grow stronger.

Exercise A: Review Your History

All people have experienced times in their lives when they've stood up for themselves and taken responsibility for their actions and times when they haven't. Try to pinpoint at least three examples when you've taken charge of your life and three times when you have not. Get out your workbook and complete the following statements for each incident. Or simply write about your feelings regarding both the positive and negative experiences in your past.

I took charge of my life when _____.

I was able to do so at that time because _____.

I didn't take responsibility for _____.

If I had to do it over again, I would _____.

Exercise B: Strengthen Your Stands

Taking charge of your life means being able to stand up for yourself. But what do you stand for? Are you someone who's honest? Do you want to let go of little bad habits, such as procrastinating? Or do you need to address more serious problems, such as drug addiction? Whether you need to stand your ground on small or large issues, you can strengthen your ability to do so by identifying your commitments. Using the space provided, or your workbook, complete the following statements:

In my relationships, I am committed to _____.

For my physical and mental health, I am committed to _____.

To ensure my safety, I am committed to _____.

If I know someone who is abusive or receiving abuse, I am committed to _____.

F. Review

What did you learn about yourself and about other people in this step?

_____

_____

What did you learn from this step that made you feel better about yourself?

_____

_____

Now, add a statement to your barometer at the end of step 10.

Once you have completed the reading and exercises for this step, both you and an adult adviser should sign below. By doing so, you are solidifying your commitment to growing stronger and safer.

Adult Adviser's Signature _____

Reader's Signature _____

> We make our decisions, and then our
> decisions turn around and make us.
>
> —F. W. Boreham

Step 7

Set Goals to Succeed

What does it take to make an Olympic champion? How do you become a successful actor, athlete, musician, or trapeze artist? In each case, self-control and self-discipline lead to success. It takes long hours and even years of practice to become successful. Champions stay calm so they can do their best. Most important, they set goals and work toward them. So can you! When you set and achieve goals, you develop self-discipline and self-esteem. You are becoming more self-confident and empowered.

Plan ahead to be successful.

By planning your future, you are also making a statement that you are someone who deserves respect and protection. Here, in step 7, you will learn to shape your future by setting goals to succeed.

A. Set Long-Term Goals

What's your goal for the future? What do you enjoy doing in your free time—drawing pictures, fixing old clocks, reading about space, or gazing at the stars? Would you like to be a professional ballplayer, a dancer, a flower shop owner, a pilot, or a rancher? Can you imagine a future in which you repair computers, become a carpenter, or attend college? A goal can help you focus on something you wish to accomplish for yourself. It can inspire you to read books, do research, and earn money to accomplish your dreams. Setting goals gives purpose to your life.

If you're not sure what interests you, volunteer to work at different jobs to learn more about a particular profession. For example, if a business in the neighborhood sounds interesting, make an appointment to see the owner and offer to help out for a month. Find out what your neighbors do, and ask them questions about their work.

Perhaps you can observe a TV repairman, an auto mechanic, or a court reporter. Most adults will be flattered if you show an interest in their profession. In other words, find a mentor. You won't know if you don't ask. Whatever your interest, look on the computer or in the library for articles and magazines on the subject.

Think of setting a long-term goal as giving yourself a target to shoot for or a destination to reach. When you aim high, you'll be surprised at the things that begin to happen. You may discover hidden talents and a whole new level of living that you never knew existed.

Having a long-term goal also puts your day-to-day efforts into perspective. Sometimes, the small things you do each day may not seem to matter much, but when you look at your everyday life from the point of view of your long-term future, then you will see how much difference your daily activities make. Setting a goal to run a marathon, for instance, gives you the incentive to keep going while running the countless miles you need to cover during training. And long-term goals can also make you more willing to sacrifice the short-term pleasures of today for the deep satisfaction of success in your future.

A Life Experience

James did poorly in grammar school because he had difficulty reading. He was shy and hated to speak in front of the class. It never occurred to him that he would grow up to be a teacher. No one could imagine a bright future for James, but one teacher took a special interest in him because he wanted to succeed. In spite of his difficulty reading, James gradually improved by putting in extra time reading out loud to himself in his room. Even though his grades remained below average, James told his teacher that one day he was going to graduate from college. James kept doing extra schoolwork and asked other students to help him. By the time he got to high school, he joined the debate team and began writing articles for the school paper. One of the best days of his life took place when his acceptance papers for college arrived. His hard work paid off as he happily headed off to earn his degree to become a teacher.

Questions to Consider

What are your goals for the future? Where do you want to be in three years, five years, or ten years? What will you give up now in order to reach an important goal for the future?

B. Set Short-Term Goals to Achieve Long-Term Success

A long-term goal is important, but in order to achieve that goal, you need to plan a series of small steps to get there. Every big project, dream, or goal can be broken down into smaller pieces that are easy to manage. It took years to construct the Empire State Building, for instance, but that project never would have been completed without the millions of small steps needed to build it brick by brick.

Short goals are those that can be accomplished quickly—sometimes in a day, a week, or a month. If you're planning to go to college, for example, a short, one-day goal might be to mail off a request for application forms. Then, you may want to set another goal of completing the application paperwork within two weeks and pick a date one month ahead as the deadline for completing essays and other materials. Or suppose your goal is to repair an engine in an old car. Your first short-term goal may be to get advice from an older mechanic or to make phone calls to find the parts you need.

Sometimes, you may need to take steps that don't seem to lead directly to your goal. For example, you want to repair the old car, as in the preceding example, but you don't have enough money to buy the necessary tools. So you get a job in a video store. Even though renting videos doesn't seem to have anything to do with old cars, you are actually moving toward your goal because the money you earn will help you accomplish your aim.

The purpose of setting a goal that can be reached quickly is that it keeps you moving in the direction you want to go. As each little accomplishment builds on the others, you reach a point where your big dreams become realities.

A Life Experience

At the age of forty-seven, Jack was an overweight smoker. When a friend had a heart attack, Jack took it as a wake-up call and made it his goal to get in shape. The first time he tried running, he could barely make it around his backyard. He set goals to achieve his dream of running a marathon. He ran three blocks, and then he upped it to six blocks and then a mile. With every

benchmark reached, Jack grew stronger and healthier. He gave up cigarettes and junk food. Jack ran his first marathon a year and a half after he started training. Then, he decided to set himself a new goal that seemed impossible: he would complete a triathlon by age fifty. He accomplished his goal.

Questions to Consider

How did Jack use short-term goals to reach his long-term objectives? How can you apply Jack's lessons to your life?

C. Exercise Your Self-Awareness

Now that you know a little about setting goals and the benefits of pursuing them, use these exercises to chart your own course to success.

Exercise A: Visualize Your Goal

Visualization can help you reach your goals. Set aside some quiet time for yourself each day. Close your eyes, and let your imagination paint a picture of your future. See yourself attending college, opening your own business, or starting a new job. Think about the sounds and sights, the feelings and experiences you will have when you accomplish your goal. Write a statement that captures your vision or spend time putting your thoughts down in your journal or workbook. Draw pictures of your goal or create a collage that captures your goal visually. Then post your statement or artwork on your mirror, desk, or closet door. Read your goal statement several times a day, or spend time looking at your artwork. If you can visualize and reinforce your goal by repeating it verbally or meditating on it visually, it will help you focus on your future.

Exercise B: Make an Action Plan

The following questions are designed to give you ideas to think about in setting your own goals. To create an action plan, write out your long-term and short-term goals in each area that you want to improve on. You don't have to plan for every single short-range goal, but if you start with at least two items, you will generate the momentum you need to take the next steps. Periodically review your action plan. Check off any items you've completed, and revise your plan with new goals as you progress.

What can I do to improve my schoolwork?

Education is important to your future. It gives you a good foundation for future success. Identify the subject you want to improve on. For example, if you want to do better in Spanish, join a Spanish club or purchase a Spanish-language tape. Ask an advanced student or bilingual citizen to help you. Teach Spanish to a young child. (A good way to learn something is to teach it.) If you want to improve your reading skills, make a commitment to read one more book a month on a subject you really enjoy. In order to improve in any subject, spend a little extra time each day working on it and be creative.

My long-term goal to improve my schoolwork: _____

My short-term goals to improve my schoolwork: _____

_____

What can I do to strengthen my spiritual life?

Everyone needs to be introspective at least some of the time. *Introspection* means taking the time to look within and make changes to help you become more positive and productive. If you know you have a tendency to be bossy, practice listening to others. Set a goal of trying not to boss anyone for a week. If you are too quiet, make yourself get involved so you have to speak up. Keep a journal and note each time you speak up. Read books on spirituality and religion. Talk to religious advisers or peers who have an active spiritual life.

Visit a local church, temple, or mosque. Remember, you are working on your future. Challenge yourself to grow stronger.

My long-term goal to improve my spiritual life: _____

My short-term goals to improve my spiritual life: _____

What can I do to improve my health?

Your health is directly related to your outlook on life, and a positive outlook is generally healthier. Be aware of the thoughts you focus on, the amount of exercise you get, the food you eat, and the chemicals (including drugs or alcohol) that you put into your body. Your actions and attitudes can help make you sick or healthy. Set small goals to improve your health, such as eliminating one kind of junk food each week. Or try to exercise ten minutes each day and gradually build up more time.

A Life Experience

Juanita had a difficult childhood, and as a teenager, she had developed arthritis in her wrists and feet. She taped her wrists to reduce the pain. A specialist said she would have to take cortisone shots for the rest of her life to control the crippling effects of the disease. She had one shot and never went back. It didn't make sense to her that she could have this disease at such a young age. She decided to take charge of her own health. She changed her diet and learned to let go of resentments toward her parents. She started exercising every day. It took several years before the flare-ups stopped. Juanita was wise enough to realize she could control her health.

My long-term goal to improve my health: _____

What can I do to improve my physical fitness?

Taking care of your body is an important part of being self-aware and street safe. A short-term goal may be to learn more about nutrition. Books can help you learn which foods to avoid or how to decrease the amount of fat you eat. You can also walk or bike to school instead of taking the bus, participate in a new sport, or join a gym class. As you take charge of your emotional health, you can do the same for your physical health.

My long-term goal to improve my physical fitness: _____

My short-term goals to improve my physical fitness: _____

_____

What can I do to improve my relationships?

When you have a misunderstanding, ask questions and listen. "We don't seem to be getting along lately. What can I do to improve our relationship?" Don't get defensive when you hear the answer. Then set a goal of improving one area at a time. Perhaps you need to do better on returning phone calls or making compromises. Honestly resolve to improve these areas and see if your actions make the relationship better. Let go of your ego; be positive, and listen to others.

My long-term goal to improve my relationships: _____

My short-term goals to improve my relationships: _____

_____

What can I do to expand my social circle?

Set a goal to meet two new people each week. Write each name on a three-by-five index card. Start an alphabetical file and jot down addresses, phone numbers, interests, hobbies, and other information.

Your new friends will remember you if you remember them. Your three-by-five cards can help you increase your network of contacts.

Caution: Everyone needs time alone to study, set goals, and dream about the future. However, it's important not to become too isolated or disconnected from reality. Think about your habits. Do you listen to too much music alone? Do you watch too much television or spend too much time on the computer? Being able to communicate with others and build a social network can ensure your success in the future. Develop networking skills at an early age so you will excel later.

My long-term goal to improve my network of support: _____

My short-term goals to improve my network of support: _____

_____

What can I do to reduce family conflicts?

If there is abuse in the family, talk to an adult you trust and get help. You can't solve that problem alone. However, bickering and anger are issues you can address. How do you feel when a parent tells you to clean your room, finish a project, or get your homework done? Is he or she taking advantage of you or trying to teach you life skills, such as being able to meet a deadline, get organized, and be responsible? If you feel the rules and chores are excessive, you need to sit down and discuss it. Setting goals and working out agreements can prevent anger and stress. This way, you avoid conflicts in the future and assignments are clear. (Consider taking a course in conflict mediation to learn how to be more effective at reducing problems. See if this course is available at your school.)

My long-term goal to reduce family conflicts: _____

My short-term goals to reduce family conflicts: _____

_____

In other areas of my life, my goals are to _____

_____

_____

_____

D. Review

What did you learn about yourself and about other people in this step?

_____

_____

What did you learn from this step that made you feel better about yourself?

_____

_____

Now, add a statement to your barometer at the end of step 10.

Once you have completed the reading and exercises for this step, both you and an adult adviser should sign below. By doing so, you are solidifying your commitment to growing stronger and safer.

Adult Adviser's Signature _____

Reader's Signature _____

Find your passion in life. If you like to swim, swim. If you
like to paint, paint. Anything that inspires you is a clear sign

of a thought or idea that you can accomplish or obtain with a little determination, resourcefulness, and creativity. Follow your heart, trust your instincts, and let yourself be inspired.

—Gina, age sixteen

Step 8

Make Connections with Others

Studies have shown that people with strong connections to others are usually healthier and safer. That fact holds true not just for individuals but for communities as well. In areas where neighbors develop strong bonds and become close to one another, crime goes down. The ability to make connections with others—the focus of step 8—can also make you more street-safe and secure.

A. Find Inspiration in Others

[[[[There is an incredible network of people in your community who can inspire you. These individuals can lift you up to a new vision of possibilities. Take risks and get involved in your community. You will discover extraordinary human beings, like the people in the following list, who are volunteering to make life better for people in the San Francisco Bay Area:

- Mary Ann Wright, mother of twelve, listened to God, who called her to "feed the hungry." She fed the homeless in Oakland, California, and founded the Mary Ann Wright Foundation (http://www.insidebayarea.com/ci_12326298? source=most_viewed).

- Fred Jackson, a community activist, inspired children through his songs and original plays.
- A. J. Jelani sponsors an annual "Christmas on the Streets" block party for underprivileged children in his neighborhood. He is a role model and mentor for kids.
- Ellen Paterson educated her community by organizing a drug task force in her city.
- Don Mitchel was given one year to live. He changed his lifestyle and now spreads the message of nonviolence and social justice.
- Helen Garcia's nephew was murdered. She now devotes her life to helping families of murdered children.
- Shirley Warner, a former teacher, educates community volunteers on how to organize, develop leadership skills, and work with difficult people.

These examples point out just a few of the outstanding people who make communities safer, healthier places to live. If you look for them, you can find people who will inspire you to fulfill your goals and become the person you want to be.

A Life Experience

Barbara's children could no longer play outside because drug dealers had taken over the neighborhood park. She was angry that police seemed ineffective in handling the problem. Instead of complaining, she got neighbors together, and they began jotting down car license numbers and descriptions of dealers and documented illegal activities. They worked with the police, and within three months, the children were back, playing in the park. Barbara's actions demonstrated the importance of connecting with others and working together to accomplish a common goal.

B. Make Positive Connections

People will support you and be there for you, but you have to show a sincere interest in them to develop good friendships. Isolation from others can pull you down and make you feel depressed or unhappy. The broader your network, the less likely you will be devastated if one or two friends disappoint you. Expect friends to upset you. We are all human beings and make mistakes. The test of real friendship is to speak up without anger, forgive others (for your sake), and move on. Learn this lesson at an early age, and you won't need counseling later.

Creating a broad network of friends can be fun and rewarding. But it is important that you make connections with people who are positive. Evaluate the people and activities you are involved in today. Are they pulling you up to a new vision or dragging you down into self-destructive behavior? Are you able to say no if you don't feel comfortable?

The people likely to pull you down include those who don't feel good about who they are becoming. They may abuse drugs or alcohol, misuse sex, or exert their power to control others. Other detrimental people may bully or belong to a self-destructive group or gang and individuals who can more subtly gossip about others and try to divide people into angry factions, spread rumors, hold a grudge, and are mean to people or animals. Regardless of what form their negativity takes, whether obvious or subtle, these people can destroy your life, and you need to cut off connections to them.

Personal progress will depend on your commitment to yourself and your ability to take charge of relationships. As you grow in self-awareness and confidence, negative people will fall away, and you can develop new, uplifting friends.

C. Ask Others for Help: Don't Isolate Yourself

The ability to ask for help is strength, not weakness. In the United States, there is the myth of the lone, rugged individual who does everything on his or her own. The reality is that no one accomplishes anything alone. Just look at the long list of credits at the end of a one-man or one-woman show. Maybe one person is in the spotlight, but there are fifty people backstage making the show possible.

If life gets tough, make contact with someone who will listen—don't isolate yourself. Turn to a trusted relative, friend, neighbor, teacher, pastor, counselor, or doctor. As you become self-aware, you are more likely to know when you hit *overload*. Share your worries with an adult and seek help. Don't wait for depression to set in; speak up. The longer you wait to get help, the longer it takes to heal.

Develop strong relationships with family, friends, and associates. We can rise above the slings and arrows of life with the support of others, but we often fail if we try to do it alone. Successful people get support because they go out and find it.

A Life Experience

Erin had gone abroad as a high school student and learned the language. After her money ran out, she decided to continue traveling. She picked up odd jobs as a waitress and interpreter whenever she could. One day, she met a writer who offered to pay her if she would help him. He was writing a book on abused women and prostitution. He needed an interpreter to take him around the city.

The night of the tour, Erin was shocked to see so many young women working as prostitutes. As the man interviewed the prostitutes, their stories had a similar pattern of abuse, molestation, and rape.

That evening had a dramatic effect on Erin. She saw hopelessness, and it fueled her own fears. She began to worry about her choices as her health and confidence started to decline. Life no longer seemed important without friends, family, or the comfort of home. She grew depressed and started taking drugs. Erin's mother insisted that she come home. Once she reconnected with her supportive family, her health improved, and soon, her outlook on life was back on track.

Don't isolate yourself.

Questions to Consider

Why do you think Erin became depressed? What difference would it have made if she had reached out sooner?

D. Honor the Rules for Relationships

As you make connections with others, you'll find it easier to maintain these connections if you honor the following basic rules for relationships:

Be Polite

As you develop respect for yourself, you will respect others. *Respect* means listening, being centered, and acknowledging other people's concerns. Practice saying "Please" and "Thank you." When adults are introduced, stand up and shake hands. When you greet someone, smile and look him or her in the eye. Give up your seat to an older adult on a bus or train. Remember, it feels good to assist others. Answer the phone and the door with courtesy. Make it a practice to listen to others without judgment. If you can't say something nice, practice the art of being quiet. You will get back double what you give to others.

Admit Mistakes and Apologize

When you are wrong, admit and apologize. No one is perfect. We all make mistakes. When you make a mistake, don't let your ego get in the way of making an apology. If you ignore errors, you can become hardened to others. If you listen to your conscience and allow yourself to feel the pain, you lift the burden of the mistake from your shoulders and increase your level of protection from your higher power. By acknowledging your mistakes and learning from them, your inner strength will increase as you become wiser.

Restore Any Broken Connections with Your Family

You and your family have a strong spiritual link to one another. If you have conflict with a family member, try to work out your problems. No one will ever care more about you than your family. Life is too short to let your anger fester. Your resentment toward someone you *love* can keep you from progressing. Deal with it! You may not be completely successful, but you need to make the effort. For better or worse, your relationship with your family cast a shadow on all your other relationships.

Caution: If your family is seriously abusive or violent, then nothing you do may have an impact. Nevertheless, you need to take responsibility for anything you have done to hurt anyone else in your family and clean up your side of the street. You may want to seek counseling, join a twelve-step group, or find other support to help you deal with your family or friends. You do not, however, need to expose yourself to further or continued abuse or put yourself in a dangerous situation.

E. Exercise Your Self-Awareness

The exercises in this step are designed to give you practical tips on how to make strong, positive connections with other people, which, in turn, can help you become stronger and safer.

Exercise A: Accentuate the Positive

Developing the ability to make connections with other people is an important part of the process of learning about you. Make a list of everyone you know, including friends, neighbors, and relatives. Put a star beside the individuals who have skills you would like to develop or exhibit behavior you would like to improve in yourself. Accentuate the positive influences in your life. Stay in touch with your *stars,* and build strong friendships with people such as those in the following example:

- James—good student, offered to help me in math, class leader
- Angela—good listener, smart, interested in others
- Marco—kind, likes people; never talks about others
- Kaila—friendly, helpful, and we have a lot in common. I will take the time to get to know her better.

Exercise B: Connect with Others in Your Neighborhood and Community

Make a difference in your neighborhood by developing relationships with the people who live close to you. Neighbors don't have to be best friends, but we all feel safer when we are surrounded by people we can call on if needed. Neighbors need to know they can call on us. Good neighbors also work together to keep their neighborhoods safe and crime free.

To begin making a difference in your neighborhood, start with these basic questions:

Do your neighbors know one another? Do you have a neighborhood group or association? Do you have a block parent program to help protect children? Is your neighborhood experiencing serious crime and drug problems, or do you have other issues like disputes over fences, dogs, or noise? Do you have community policing and neighborhood watch programs? Does the city offer a community cleanup day and help to get rid of graffiti? Are there programs for seniors and children in the area? Who is your community representative? What other resources are available to residents?

Contact local resources to answer your questions. Look on your city webpage for contact information about police, community organizations, and local representative for help. Visit the police station, and speak to someone about community outreach programs.

Ask one or more neighbors to help. Once you research your community resources, write them down, make copies, and pass them out to neighbors. While you are distributing information, you can, at the same time, conduct a neighborhood survey. Or while you're making the rounds, ask neighbors to join you in addressing problems or working on a project, such as a cleanup day.

Find out what concerns your neighbors. Conduct a survey in your neighborhood. Here are some suggested questions to ask your neighbors.

How to Conduct a Survey:

Make a list of three questions for neighbors.

What is your biggest concern about our neighborhood?
Have you been a victim of crime?
Will you help bring neighbors together?

Consider leaving a note on neighbors' doors to inform them that you'll be conducting the survey. Then, when you go out door-to-door, put your survey on a clipboard so you'll look *official*. Introduce yourself, let them know you are a neighbor, and ask for just a few minutes of their time. Leave a note for those who are not at home so they'll know what to expect when you try them again. Think about what you will do if someone slams the door in your face. How will you handle a rude neighbor? Will you quit or find a way to succeed? You may discover areas of your character you need to develop, such as patience and persistence.

Choose a project. After you have completed the survey, bring "I will help" neighbors together as a planning group. Plan a meeting or social event, such as a barbecue or potluck, to discuss concerns. (Taking this initiative is a great way to develop your skills as well as to meet your neighbors.) Don't let the neighborhood meeting end without a plan of action, such as choosing a date for a neighborhood cleanup day, a garden-planting project, or a child-safety event. Delegate and invite a representative from the police or fire department to drop by your meeting or invite them to your block party. Consider having children participate in activities. Ask neighbors to help, and seek advice from informed residents. (For more ideas, check www.safekidsnow.com and your local library for a copy of the book *Safe Homes, Safe Neighborhoods: Stopping Crime Where You Live* from Nolo Press.)

Move beyond your neighborhood. Suppose you see a problem in the larger community, beyond your neighborhood that needs to be addressed. Perhaps you know of children in need of clothes, food, or gifts for the holidays. Or maybe a pedestrian crosswalk needs to be improved or traffic lights installed. Start a campaign to address the problem. You don't need permission, only the will to help.

Tips for community projects. These ideas may help you get started on your project:

- Research the issue that concerns you. Call your local newspaper or community representative about contacts who can help. Seek advice.
- Find out if anyone is filling the need or working on the problem already so you can join forces with an existing group instead of having to reinvent the wheel.
- Invite a few friends to help with a planning meeting.
- Print a flyer to announce meetings or let people know how they can contribute. (Flyers can be printed inexpensively, especially if you have access to a computer.)
- Go door-to-door collecting items for your donation project, such as clothes, food, toys, and so on, or signatures for your petition or campaign.
- Make a presentation to local civic groups, and ask them to help.

F. Review

What did you learn in this step about yourself and about other people?

_____

_____

What did you learn from this step that made you feel better about yourself?

_____

_____

Now, add a statement to your barometer at the end of step 10.

Once you have completed the reading and exercises for this step, both you and an adult adviser should sign below. By doing so, you are solidifying your commitment to growing stronger and safer.

Adult Adviser's Signature _____

Reader's Signature _____

> Never doubt that a small group of committed citizens can change the world; indeed, it's the only thing that ever has.
>
> —Margaret Mead

Step 9

Find Your Inner Power

The story of *The Wizard of Oz* offers an illustration of the importance of finding your inner power. As the story goes, Dorothy was in the mythical Land of Oz but wanted desperately to go home to Kansas. She headed down the yellow brick road to find the wise wizard. She met a scarecrow who wanted to join her so he could get a brain. It wasn't long before they met the tin man, who asked to join them because he wanted a heart. The cowardly lion decided to join the trio because he wanted courage. After a challenging journey, they approached the wizard. He told the scarecrow, tin man, and lion that their actions demonstrated they already possessed a heart, a brain, and courage. And Dorothy always had the power to go home by clicking her heels together; as the good witch Glenda explained, "It was inside you all along." Dorothy and her friends had been looking for some outer person to give them what they already possessed inside.

Just like the characters in Oz, you too possess inner power. The lesson Dorothy learned and the message for you to remember is this: Don't look for a wizard, guru, doctor, lawyer, or therapist to give you what you need. Learn to use your own power to take care of yourself.

Use step 9 to understand how to find your inner power to become more self-aware, street safe, and empowered.

A. Seek Self-Control

Human beings need internal control to grow strong and safe. Most parents use external controls to help a child with rules, boundaries, and limitations. If a child gets out of line, there are consequences: a spanking, a time-out, or a loss of privileges. If teens get out of control, the police use laws, curfews, community services, teen courts, or school detention. The last resort is juvenile court, juvenile hall, the state youth authority, or ultimately, jail or prison.

External controls, however, have limitations. As soon as that outside control is lifted, it no longer has power. Only when the external control becomes internalized does it have any effect. In other words, the law or rule that comes from the outside must be accepted and incorporated into a person on the inside, or else it makes no difference.

That difference between inner and outer motivation explains why many criminals return to jail. Think about it. If someone commits a crime and goes to prison, he or

Challenge yourself.

she will be prevented from doing more crime as long as the cell doors are locked. As soon as the doors are unlocked and the prisoner is released, however, that outside control disappears. The person can go right back into criminal behavior. Then, the criminal gets caught and gets sent back to prison, and the whole vicious cycle starts all over again. It is only when the criminal makes a decision to change—that is, an internal decision to change—that this cycle can be broken.

The same system holds true for children and teens. Conscientious parents use external controls to teach children how to behave when they are small, but gradually, parents expect the children to behave and follow rules on their own without the threat of punishment. They want them to understand and follow the rules so their behavior is safe regardless of whether the parent or punishment is around or not.

For example, when a young child strikes out or tries to grab a toy from someone, the parent will pull the child's hands back and say, "No! No!" When the child hits someone in the sandbox, the parent may put the child in time-out and say, "Hitting is not okay." By the time the child is four or five, the parents expect him or her to know that hitting others is not acceptable. They expect the internal controls of the child's own conscience to restrain him or her, not the threat of external punishment.

Basically, when you depend on internal controls to direct your behavior, you are demonstrating self-control. And self-control is key to expressing your inner power. Sometimes, it may seem as if an out-of-control bully or an angry, violent person has the upper hand over others, but bullies wither and run away when they are confronted by strong, centered people who don't back down. That's the true meaning of inner power—being centered and showing self-control regardless of what others do.

A Life Experience

Jackie's parents were nonsmokers, and they began talking to her at an early age about the health problems associated with smoking. When Jackie turned twelve, however, some of her friends offered her a cigarette. Jackie turned them down politely, saying, "No, thanks. I'm not interested in smoking."

A Life Experience

Joseph was only twelve years old when he joined a gang. He vandalized property, attacked and fought with rival gang members, and participated in drive-by shootings. As Joseph says today, "Street gangs entice young members with the illusion of fast living and power." At age eighteen, he almost lost his life when a bullet ripped through his chest. During his three-month rehabilitation, Joseph reflected on the choices he had made in his life. "I saw my family, my brothers, sisters, and cousins. They were so sad and worried."

Joseph decided to change his life and stop letting the other gang members determine his behavior. He regained pride in his Mexican culture and made a strong commitment to God.

Today, he works with kids at risk and teaches respect for others, self-empowerment, and appreciation of nature. He coaches sports, encourages discipline, and promotes effective methods for teens to keep away from violence. He hopes to open a residence for kids who have suffered the effects of violence.

Questions to Consider

How did Jackie show that her parents' rules had become her own? What decisions did Joseph make that shaped his life both positively and negatively? How did Jackie and Joseph express their inner power?

B. Tap the Power of Belief

In a survey of 269 doctors, a remarkable 99 percent said they were convinced that religious belief could heal. In fact, that's 20 percent higher than the percentage of the general public that recognizes this phenomenon.

Why do doctors feel this way? "It's because we've seen the power of belief," says Dr. Herbert Benson, author of *Timeless Healing*, who offers scientific evidence that faith has helped cure medical conditions including asthma, ulcers, heart failure, diabetes, and all forms of pain. "We see it all the time, and we can't deny it," Dr. Benson continues. "We have scientific data showing that people who use self-help, relaxation, nutrition, exercise, and belief can reduce their visits to doctors by 30% to 60%." For more information check out Dr. Herbert Benson's book, Timeless Healing: https://www.amazon.com/Timeless-Healing-Herbert-Benson/dp/0684831465

The reality is that your inner beliefs have enormous power to shape your outer experiences and circumstances. But what do you believe in? As stated throughout this book, only you can answer this deeply personal question. Sooner or later, however, you will have to recognize that there is something beyond your limited consciousness that is greater than you are as an individual.

You may look to nature to learn this lesson. For instance, earthquakes, hurricanes, and tornadoes all have greater power than you. Or you may learn it through the examples of people like Gandhi or Martin Luther King Jr., who believed so strongly in the power of nonviolence that they were able to change the societies in which they lived. If you are willing, you can discover that making a connection to your Creator is the surest path to finding your inner power.

C. Use Inner Power Wisely

Any power we possess, whether it's our ability to hear or to drive a car, can be used or misused. If we misuse our ears—perhaps by listening to loud music too often—we'll eventually grow deaf, as many rock stars have learned to their regret. If we drive cars safely, they'll get us to where we want to go. But if we're reckless, we'll cause accidents, injury, or even death. This same rule holds true for the inner power we possess. It can be used wisely or foolishly, positively or negatively.

It's also important that you avoid confusing talent for inner power. In our celebrity-driven culture, some young people may believe that actors, singers, and musicians are powerful because their talents earn millions. Their bank accounts, however, don't equate to inner power. In fact, sometimes, people who seem to have it all can feel they have no control over their lives. Inner power really comes from showing self-control, making a connection to the Creator, and using our talents to help others. If we misuse our gifts to mistreat or control others, we'll hurt ourselves in the long run.

An important part of developing your inner power and resiliency is to challenge yourself. Yes, when you take on a new challenge, you will have problems to solve, difficult people to face, and obstacles to overcome, but there are also unexpected rewards. Give your inner power a chance to grow. You can improve your patience, persistence, and determination. Get involved, and you can experience it for yourself!

A Life Experience

Jim didn't like his teacher because he felt he was being picked on. During the semester, he was criticized and sent to the principal's office twice. He felt he was being singled out when he had to do extra work. Jim avoided the teacher. When he was given a low grade, he was angry and depressed.

Questions to Consider

How could Jim have used his inner power to improve his relationship with the teacher? What would you have done differently?

A Life Experience

Jason, a senior, alerted the media about the run-down conditions and lack of safety at his high school. He had tried unsuccessfully to get the school board to take action, so he called news outlets. The media found broken toilets, protruding nails, rusted locks, and a broken fire door that had been chained for five years. The media's focus on the school forced officials to fix the problems. Jason, as student body president, said, "If the students have to go to school like this every day, they are going to believe this is what the world is about—that there's no hope. What does it say about the future of this country?"

Questions to Consider

What do you think motivated Jason to step out of the crowd and make a difference at his school? Why didn't he quit when the school board ignored him?

A Life Experience

James and Chris are students at a high school in California. They were concerned about the school budget problems that threatened to eliminate music, arts, and sports programs. They gathered three hundred signatures, circulated fliers, and scheduled a meeting with parents and the principal. The boys were able to get parents and administrators to work together peacefully to find solutions.

Questions to Consider

How did James and Chris help future students? How do you think the boys were able to get the parents and administrators to work together?

A Life Experience

A group of high school boys in a low-income neighborhood decided to help the community. They went door-to-door and offered to tutor elementary children after school three days a week. They received recognition from the community for their work with children.

Questions to Consider

Why would a group of high school boys want to help tutor elementary students? How do you think it made them feel to get involved in this way?

D. Exercise Your Self-Awareness

These exercises are designed to help you discover the power you have within and use it in a way that benefits others.

Exercise A: Show Your Self-Control

Keep track of what upsets you. Be aware of how you react to other people and how they react to you. Did your behavior make a difficult situation better or worse? How many times a week do you feel upset or depressed? Can you bounce back? Do you keep grudges or solve problems? Write out your answers to these questions in your journal or notebook. Review your notes every few weeks.

Exercise B: Express Your Inner Power

An easy way to express or demonstrate your inner power to the outside world is by doing something to make a positive impact on others. Why not start with your school? Is there a drug problem? Is property being stolen, or are students being harassed? Write an article for the school paper. Ask questions of the students. Do students feel safe? If not, start a safety campaign. Go to the school authorities and suggest a student-safety council to research problems and make recommendations to improve school security. Do a survey to find out the extent of the problem. Promote a poster or essay contest to help educate administrators, parents, and students. Tap your creativity to show the strength of your inner power.

E. Review

What did you learn about yourself and about other people in this step?

_____

_____

What did you learn from this step that made you feel better about yourself?

_____

_____

Now, add a statement to your barometer at the end of step 10.

Once you have completed the reading and exercises for this step, both you and an adult adviser should sign below. By doing so, you are solidifying your commitment to growing stronger and safer.

Adult Adviser's Signature _____

Reader's Signature _____

> Men are anxious to improve their circumstances, but are unwilling to improve themselves; they therefore remain bound.
>
> —James Allen

Step 10

Discover Your Unlimited Potential

Discovering your unlimited potential is a journey of faith, yet it is not a matter of *blind* faith. Rather, this journey is one where you can follow a clearly marked path toward greater self-awareness. And you have already taken many steps on that path. If you have honestly put forth the effort to complete the previous nine steps in this guidebook, you have ignited the engine that will launch you into a limitless future. Here in step 10, you will see how you can go further than you have ever dreamed possible.

A. Reach for the Stars

When you hear the words *unlimited potential*, what image comes to mind? Do you think of astronauts traveling to the moon? Or do you think of a sports star with a bright future ahead? The Merriam-Webster Dictionary says synonyms for *unlimited* include *boundless, infinite, unrestricted,* and *vast.* As for *potential*, one definition reads, "A latent excellence or ability that may or may not be developed."

Now, what do these words mean to you?

Do you want to develop your vast, latent abilities? Or will you ignore your hidden talents and go through life without fully discovering your potential? The choice is really yours. No one can force you. Only you can make the choice and dedicate the energy needed to reach for the stars—wherever you see them.

Your life's journey will be unique, and it is shaped by the choices you make every day. You can move up toward self-understanding and awareness or move down into self-denial and delusion. Your spiritual journey can be rewarded beyond your wildest expectations. No one knows the future, but you can know that your higher power has an exciting plan for your life.

A (Few) Life Experiences

Basketball player Michael Jordan was cut from his high school team before he became one of the greatest champions in the game. Albert Einstein failed math in grammar school. Abraham Lincoln lost numerous elections before he finally won the presidency. And Helen Keller became a well-known public speaker even though she was born blind and deaf. All these people went beyond the limitations others imposed on them in order to realize their unlimited potential.

Question to Consider

Do you know anyone who has gone beyond their limits to achieve their dreams?

B. Make Up Your Mind to Succeed

Perhaps you have heard the old saying "You are what you eat," which means that the things you take into your body will determine how you look and feel. When it comes to reaching for your unlimited potential, that phrase may be changed to "You are what you *think*." Your thoughts determine your actions, and your actions define your life. You'll find people who live by this truth in every arena, from those who pursue a spiritual discipline to those who grow businesses or excel in the arts.

If you believe something is possible, then you will do everything to support that belief. But if you are negative and believe something is impossible, then you will act accordingly. In the words of carmaker Henry Ford, "Think you can or think you can't—either way you will be right."

So if you don't believe you can do math, you are right. And if you don't believe you can become a better student, athlete, or family member, you'll be right again. By the same token, if you *do* believe in yourself, you'll be right about that too! The reality is what *you* believe. We all fulfill our vision with what we think we are worth. If we fail to have faith, we miss the exciting opportunities our higher power has in store for us. We miss the chance to become self-aware, and we certainly won't be street safe or feel empowered.

Have you ever heard of a placebo? These substances are used in scientific tests when some patients are given sugar pills, or placebos, instead of medication. Studies have shown that the sugar pills sometimes help the patients as much as the real medicine. For example, in one study, a group of participants who suffered from sleep loss were given what they thought was a new sleeping pill. Most of the patients reported fantastic improvements and wanted a prescription for the new medication. In reality, each of those patients had been given a placebo, but each believed that the pills were making them sleep better. Because of what they thought in their minds, their bodies responded. That shows how powerful our minds and thoughts can be.

Remember, your path in life is determined by what *you* believe. We are all incredibly spiritual beings who can overcome anything and let our inner light shine. Having faith that we can accomplish any goal takes us out of a self-imposed box of limitations. So make up your mind to succeed and begin to discover your unlimited potential.

C. Define Your Spiritual Path

The surest way to tap into your unlimited potential is to listen to your Creator's plan for your life. But how do you do that? You must develop a bond with your higher power and be willing to change as you learn spiritual lessons.

Because we are imperfect, consider attending religious services. Just as we need instructions to make the VCR work and to understand a computer, so too do we need guidance to help us find inner peace. A religious group can give you a sense of family with people who share the same values. As you get closer to your Creator, you can begin to discover what you need to work on. You will understand why you need to be thankful for what you have, and you will find support to get past the difficult times.

A religious group should offer a clear purpose and principles to live by. It should also help strengthen family bonds and encourage members to reach out to one another. It should not, however, cut you off from your support network or take over your life and livelihood. That is what cults do, not groups that are legitimately interested in helping you define your own spiritual path. So beware! There are bullies in every walk of life. Religious groups have controlling leaders just as law firms have corrupt lawyers, hospitals have unethical doctors, and corporations have greedy business executives. Use your instincts and trust your wisdom to see the difference between leaders who try to control behavior and those who try to develop spiritually strong and centered people. It's up to you to define your spiritual path; don't leave it to anyone else.

If you are not quite ready to join a religious organization, consider studying the Ten Commandments or reading other spiritual material on your own. These basic rules have been strengthening people around the world for thousands of years. The Ten Commandments are powerful guidelines that have inspired and changed people's lives. We can all find happiness and a purpose for our lives by taking steps to learn and be guided by our conscience. See if you can find any parallels between these suggestions and the Ten Commandments.

The Ten Suggestions for a Happy Life

1. *Trust* your conscience (inner power), which can keep you free and independent. Observe behavior but do not react to false messengers who try to pull you down and control your behavior.
2. *Sit quietly* and listen as you look within yourself for guidance. Do not follow false role models, such as movie, television, or sports stars because human beings are imperfect. Love your Creator, and keep the Creator's laws, or your children can suffer without developing their own identity.
3. *Think* before you speak. Use self-discipline in the words you choose, being careful not to offend others.
4. *Take time* each week to renew yourself. Meditate and reflect on what you have accomplished and how you need to change to improve your quality of life.
5. *Respect* your parents. Understand they are not perfect. They have given you life, but they may be unaware of your needs. Your grandparents may have been unaware of your parents' needs. Put your trust in God, and grow in self-awareness.

6. *Learn* to handle anger, or it will handle you. Anger is a negative energy. Harbor no malice or desire to harm another in your heart. Practice forgiveness so you can have peace.

7. *You are a unique and special individual.* Think about the consequences before considering a sexual relationship. Sex creates a spiritual bond between the participants. Ask for guidance in your choice of a mate.

8. *Beware!* Do not take anything that doesn't belong to you. If you rationalize negative behavior, it becomes easier to take from others, and that puts you on a self-destructive path. There are negative consequences for bad choices, such as addiction, poor health, and loss of relationships.

9. *Be careful* not to spread lies or gossip. It comes back in painful ways. People will not trust you, and you may become a target for others.

10. *Caution!* Jealousy and envy are emotions that pull you down. Resist filling your mind with negative thoughts and focus on being thankful for what you have. Positive energy strengthens you as you become a spiritually centered person.

D. Exercise Your Self-Awareness

You can find your unique path and discover your unlimited potential if you are willing to look for it. These exercises will help you see the barriers that can block your progress as well as the vision that can keep you going.

Exercise A: Face Fears First

Having a fearful thought is not bad. It's only when you let your fears paralyze you that they have a negative effect on your life. Sometimes, a fear is simply an excuse to prevent you from moving forward. In this exercise, think about the excuses you may be using to avoid fulfilling your potential. If you face your fears first, you can get them out of the way, and then there's nothing to stop you.

Finish the following sentences to reveal any hidden fears. In the first blank of the sentence, write out your fear (or excuse), and in the second blank, write your goal or dream. Once you see your fears clearly, you can address the specific problem you have identified or simply decide to let go of the issue. For instance, if you fear a lack of money, then you can look into getting a part-time job or focus on saving money. Or if you fear that others will ridicule your work, you can choose to ignore them.

Examples

If only I had enough money, *I could* start my own business.

If only I could go to college, *I would be* successful.

If only my parents supported me, *I'd have become a* star.

Now fill out these statements for yourself:

If only I had _____

I could _____

If only I could _____

I would _____

If only _____

I'd have become a _____

Exercise B: Envision Your Future

Thomas Edison was once asked how he came up with so many inventions, such as the light bulb and phonograph. He replied, "It is because I never think in words. I think in pictures." Take some time to imagine your future by painting a picture of it in your mind. Then draw out the image in your notebook or make a photo collage of it. Once you envision your future, set specific goals (see step 7) to make it possible.

Exercise C: Review Your Progress

This exercise can help you see the progress you have made throughout the ten steps you have just completed. Write out your thoughts about each statement and then file it away for future reference to evaluate your progress. If you don't know the answer now, you will discover it as you continue to grow. Trust yourself and be patient.

In what ways are you unique? _____

Why is pain an important part of life? _____

How should you handle anger and resentment? _____

Why do you need to be spiritually centered? _____

What is the difference between someone who can follow instructions and a person who is a follower? _____

What is the difference between being self-absorbed and being self-aware? _____

Why should you be on time, keep your room clean, or have a clean space to study in? _____

Why is it important to treat others with respect? _____

How can your instincts protect you? _____

How can you take charge of your life? _____

How does self-awareness help you become responsible for your actions? _____

How can setting goals help you plan for your future? _____

How can reaching out to others help you find your
way? _____

Where can you find the power to live life to the
fullest? _____

How can you discover your potential? _____

What do you want in your future? _____

You now have a clearer vision of what it takes to discover your identity
and your unlimited potential. No one can force you, intimidate you,
or threaten you to take charge of your life. The desire to do so can
only come from within. These ten steps can help you start your
exciting journey. Be patient with yourself and others. Have faith
that your Creator can show you the way as you prepare yourself for
a spectacular future. Understand that temptation is all around you.
Think before you make a decision that can change your life. If you
fall, remember your Creator is there to guide you back on the path.
Life can be an exciting struggle to find inner peace. Enjoy the ride
with a happy heart and you can make others happy. May you be
blessed and find peace within yourself.

E. Review

What did you learn about yourself and about other people in this step?

_____

_____

What did you learn from this step that made you feel better about
yourself?

_____

_____

Now, add a statement to your barometer at the end of step 10.

Once you have completed the reading and exercises for this step, both you and an adult adviser should sign below. By doing so, you are solidifying your commitment to growing stronger and safer.

Adult Adviser's Signature _____

Reader's Signature _____

> Our deepest fear is not that we are inadequate. Our deepest fear is that we are powerful beyond measure. It is our light, not our darkness, that frightens us. We ask ourselves, who am I to be brilliant, gorgeous, talented, and fabulous? Actually, who are you not to be? You are a child of God. Your playing small doesn't serve the world. There is nothing enlightened about shrinking so that other people won't feel insecure around you. We are born to make manifest the glory of God that is within us. It's not just in some of us; it's in everyone. And as we let our light shine, we unconsciously give other people permission to do the same. As we are liberated from our own fear, our presence automatically liberates others.

> —Excerpt from *A Return to Love* by Marianne Williamson

Instructions: Write a statement below in your own words that best expresses your attitude after you have read and completed each step and its exercises. See the examples for ideas on wording.

Attitude Barometer #2

True power comes from within.
I am self-aware and use self-control
to find my higher purpose

_____

_____

_____

_____

_____

_____

_____

_____

I often feel lonely and depressed.

Step 1 – Exercise A

(and review exercise for all steps)

I will be successful. I am taking
responsibility for my future.

_____

_____

_____

_____

_____

_____

_____

I don't care who I hurt. I don't even
care about me.

Review

Street-Safe Tips for Teens

Your actions and reactions can keep you safe.

- Treat others with respect, and they are more likely to treat you with respect.
- Don't overreact to bullies; walk away or report violent behavior.
- Practice self-control; stay cool, calm, and collected to handle difficult people and dangerous situations.
- Walk or run away if you don't feel safe.
- Develop your self-confidence and self-awareness to stay alert.
- Revenge is self-defeating. Channel your anger in a positive way to stay street safe.
- Handle emotional pain as a learning experience, or it can cause fear, anxiety, and social isolation.
- Connect with well-balanced and centered friends.
- Pay attention to your intuition and instincts to help you stay alert and safe.
- Negative secrets make you vulnerable to abuse and addictions. Find a trusted adult and share your problems.

- You have the power to take charge of your future. Use your head, not just your heart, before you make any life-changing decisions.
- Set high standards to grow healthy and stay safe.
- Develop good relationships and create a network of supportive friends.
- Becoming self-aware can keep you safe at home, in school, and in your neighborhood.
- Help others create a network of safety as you develop your people skills.
- Know that you can make a difference in other people's lives by working with them.

Step into the future

with self-confidence and courage.

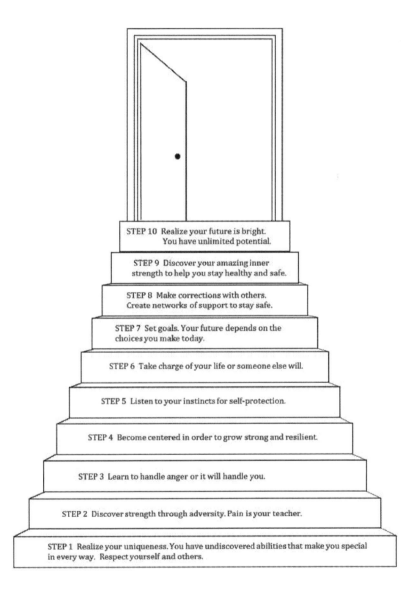

STEP 10 Realize your future is bright.
You have unlimited potential.

STEP 9 Discover your amazing inner
strength to help you stay healthy and safe.

STEP 8 Make corrections with others.
Create networks of support to stay safe.

STEP 7 Set goals. Your future depends on the
choices you make today.

STEP 6 Take charge of your life or someone else will.

STEP 5 Listen to your instincts for self-protection.

STEP 4 Become centered in order to grow strong and resilient.

STEP 3 Learn to handle anger or it will handle you.

STEP 2 Discover strength through adversity. Pain is your teacher.

STEP 1 Realize your uniqueness. You have undiscovered abilities that make you special
in every way. Respect yourself and others.

Part 2

Empowerment Parenting Guide for Parents and Adults

This section in part 2 can help parents and adults reinforce the ten steps in part 1's section for teens. As the reader and adult work together with part 1, they can use part 2 to further strengthen positive values and to discover other ways of keeping young people safe.

How to Use this Guide for Parents and Adults

(You can use this guide to help a child of any age. We use *teen* to keep the text easy to read.)

The *Empowerment Parenting* guide is written to help parents and adults interact with young people in a positive and supportive way. This "seed-planting" guide can also assist adults and group leaders in discussing difficult topics, such as how to react to anger, pain, and negative experiences. As movies, magazines, videos, television, and the Internet bombard teens with confusing messages, it becomes more important than ever to give young people a clear understanding of how to avoid self-destructive behavior.

This ten-step guide offers the opportunity to encourage young people to grow stronger from within as they learn how to become centered. In addition, you can share your family values to wake up a preteen or teen's self-awareness. A self-aware teen is more mature and more likely to make positive choices. Learning these steps early in life can help teens develop a strong foundation of courage and character, which in turn can help them reach their full potential.

We suggest that adults read each step in the preceding section before or with teens prior to using the corresponding steps in the adults' section (part 2). The adult steps contain important information and ideas for adults to keep young people safe. Teens can work on one step per week alone or with an adult, depending on age.

What the Teen Reader Will Need

- a specific time and place each week to read each step
- a notebook (or special journal) and pen or pencil for completing the exercises
- adult encouragement and commitment to see it through
- follow-up sessions for self-evaluation exercises and goal setting

It will be up to the adults in a teen's life to help the teen understand that self-evaluation is an important part of growing up and becoming responsible. When *you* think self-awareness and self-discipline are important, so will your teenager. The greatest gift you can give teenagers is to listen to them and share your thoughts without judgment. If you listen to your young children and teens now, they will listen to you later. (See "The Listening Chair" in part 2, step 2.)

Step 1

Recognize How Special You Are

Discipline without freedom is tyranny; freedom without discipline is chaos.

—Cullen Hightower

Today's parents seem to have more to do but less time to do it. Sometimes, the job of parenting feels overwhelming. But you don't have to spend endless hours with teens to have an impact. You do, however, need to give them solid support so they can grow into strong, centered, independent, and street-safe adults.

You need to help teens recognize how special they are. That is the goal of step 1.

Everyone has hidden abilities and talents. Reinforce the idea that each teen is unique. Avoid insults and put-downs, as they serve no positive purpose. No parent wants to look back and say, "I wish I had done something before my child … joined a gang, took drugs, got arrested, became violent, got pregnant, joined a cult, or became a victim." (You can fill in the blank with fears parents often discuss.) Teens who feel loved and respected develop self-awareness, which allows them to grow into the people they are meant to be. Strong and self-aware teens are less likely to become victims, to victimize others, or to make choices that are self-destructive.

A. Help Your Teen Feel Special

You are the most important influence in your teen's life, but don't take love between a parent and teen for granted. Build your relationship as you support your teen to grow in maturity.

Encourage your teen to express opinions. When you and your teen are in a comfortable mood at home or out to dinner, ask questions and listen to his or her views. Don't challenge or get angry. Listen, even if you disagree. Discuss your views calmly. If you listen when children are young, they will listen to you when they are teenagers. Even if your record on listening wasn't so great when they were younger, it's not too late to start. You may need to be more patient, but you can rebuild communication if you are willing to work at it. Remember, listening to your teen's opinions does not mean you have to go along with them. You can listen and still hold the line on family rules and boundaries.

Plan time together, and focus on one child at a time. Find ways to let teens know you love them. Cook a special meal, take them to a fun event, go for a walk in the park, and give them frequent hugs. A teen who feels special and loved will treat you and others with respect.

Be patient. You may not think teens are paying attention, but they are learning from you. You are the one your teenager wants to please. You are his or her role model and mentor.

A Life Experience

Caroline and a friend went shopping for a birthday present with her mother. The girls walked into the store as the mother paused to look at something in the window. Suddenly, she heard the shopkeeper yell,

"I don't want you kids stealing from me! Get out of my store!" The mother was surprised by the outburst and asked what had happened.

The shopkeeper apologized, saying, "Sorry, I thought they were alone."

On the way home, the angry girls discussed how they might go back and "rip him off." The mother agreed the shopkeeper's behavior was unfair, but she pointed out that he had obviously had problems in the past. It took a few minutes before the girls agreed that shoplifting would be a bad idea because they knew there were always consequences for doing the wrong thing. She reminded them to take care of their conscience and told them they would get stronger if they let the store owner's anger roll off them. Caroline's mother also asked them to recognize that the angry outburst was his problem, not theirs.

Questions to Consider

How did Caroline's mother show the girls they were special? What would you have done in this situation?

Support their dreams. Imagine your son is small for his age, but he dreams of becoming a fullback in the National Football League, or your daughter wears a size-12 shoe and wants to be a ballerina. Encourage them regardless, and let teens know they *can* accomplish their dreams. Your support is an important part of developing a can-do attitude and becoming self-aware. You can always steer them toward other activities that may be more appropriate for their size or talents, but you don't need to squash their fantasies. It's better to allow them to try out for different activities and discover their true passions for themselves than for you to put them down for daring to dream. Don't discourage teens, or they may stop dreaming.

Tell teens how much you love them. Your opinion is critical to their emotional development.

A Life Experience

At age eight, Josie hated to read in front of the class. She often stumbled over words, and the teacher seemed annoyed. Children would giggle. At her fourth-grade graduation, each child received a ribbon stating the subject in which he or she excelled. Nancy's ribbon read "Best Speller," Ann was the "Best Reader," and Barry was the "Best Printer." Josie heard her name and shyly walked up to the principal to receive her ribbon. The teacher announced Josie was the "Most Patient." Several classmates snickered, but Josie turned to find her mother smiling and giving her reassuring nods. Josie knew that being *patient* must be okay because her mother thought she was a winner.

On the way home, Mother explained that patience was the most important trait anyone could have because with patience, you could succeed at anything. She assured her that was a special gift. It didn't seem important what the other children thought because her mother thought she was special.

Questions to Consider

Why is your child special? When was the last time you told your child that he or she had exceptional or hidden talents?

B. Monitor the Media's Impact on Self-Esteem

The media has enormous power to influence children and teens. Young people are like sponges that soak up the values society glorifies. A child's perception can be blurred by Hollywood images. Teens often worship personalities that society promotes as ideal. In the process, they may diminish themselves and feel they are inadequate or they don't measure up.

If you are going to help teens recognize they are special, which is one step in the process of helping empower them, you need to discuss good and bad media influences.

Hollywood sends confusing messages, such as to be a better person, you must have the *look*. Girls may feel they need to be thin and sexy. Some girls even try to control their weight to the point that they become anorexic. Movies and magazine can encourage young girls to use their sexuality in order to be popular. Girls may dress in provocative ways to be noticed. Boys may feel they need to be stronger with bulging muscles. The macho young man is encouraged to fight for his honor and make sexual conquests.

Immature teens can go to extremes by trying to change their physical appearance through dieting, steroids, plastic surgery, bodybuilding, hair coloring, makeup, tattoos, body piercing, or sexy clothes—all just to be noticed or fit in. Teens are struggling to feel good about who they are and looking for acceptance. They are trying to discover their identities and self-esteem. Parents need to discuss media images and help teens understand that self-esteem comes from within. It is not something you can purchase.

Many busy parents don't realize that movies, television, videos, or the Internet can become a child's moral teacher as society has gradually accepted casual sex, foul language, and abusive, violent behavior. Immature preteens and teens should be protected from explicit information. It is up to you to evaluate your child's maturity and decide what is age-appropriate information. (See the discussion on the "*maturity flip*" in part 1, step 2.)

If your child uses a computer, find out what he or she is doing and who his or her friends are. Find out what information is coming into his or her email. You may add a child-protector chip to your computer. (Check with your computer store or search the Internet for more information.)

Take the time to check out movies and videos. Immature teens should not be exposed to sexual and violent content. With your guidance, you can strengthen them so they won't become confused. Teens need to develop at their own pace and discover their own identities so the media will not adversely affect them.

Share your thoughts and values. Discuss media images with them calmly. Your teen will begin to reflect your ideas and values. Encourage children of all ages to discuss what they see in movies and on TV. Help them understand that sex is used to sell everything from soap to cars. The media is a moneymaking business. It plays on the public's weakness for sexual images to sell products. You can't change the appetite of the public, but you can help teens understand the dynamics of the market and monitor how they spend their time.

In addition to recognizing the effect of violent media, parents must also contend with violent music. The lyrics of violent songs may make a teen feel better and drown out emotional pain. However, when an immature person is struggling to find his or her identity, he or she may become vulnerable to hypnotic rhythms and self-destructive ideas.

A Life Experience

Jason was thirteen years old when he hung himself with an amplifier cord while listening to the Sex Pistols. His father blamed himself and his son's alcohol use for his death.

A Life Experience

Ray's fifteen-year-old son shot himself as he listened to shock rocker Marilyn Manson. The father blamed the song for his son's death. The lyrics state, "One shot and the world gets smaller. Let's jump upon the sharp swords ... There is an exit here." After the boy's death, a recording executive observed, "The music may echo a teenager's emotional state." And Dr. Frank Palumbo of the American Academy of Pediatrics stated, "Teenagers become absorbed in songs they believe help better define them during this rocky transition to adulthood."

Questions to Consider

How much TV does your teen watch? Do you decide what movies are appropriate to see, or does your teen decide? Do you own violent videos? Does your teen listen to violent music? Do you think violence in the media should be reduced? Are you willing to speak up and get involved?

C. Take Action to Protect Young People

These action ideas are designed to help you if you are concerned about reducing the media's impact on young people in order to bolster their self-esteem:

- Get together with other parents and write letters to offending television sponsors. Form a group and start a letter-writing campaign. It has been proven that sponsors listen to consumers. One letter of complaint is translated into a hundred angry viewers.
- Do some homework on the Internet or at the library to find organized groups that are working to improve the media.
- Join a national media-monitoring group and get on their mailing list (see resource list).

~~~

Use this space to jot down your thoughts about this step. Include positive action steps you can use with your teenager.

Step 2

Discover Strength through Pain

The outward behavior of a man is at once the sign and proof of the inner state.

—Mahatma Gandhi

There is a great temptation to overprotect our children from emotional pain. Although it can be hard to go through, you are not doing your teen any favors if you prevent him or her from dealing with difficult situations. That is why step 2 is so important! You can help teens discover strength through pain. You can't fight teenagers' battles, but you can help them learn how to grow stronger. When teens solve their own problems, it builds their confidence to handle the next problem that comes along.

A. Practice Role-Playing to Strengthen Teens

Mean-spirited behavior by peers is one common type of pain teens experience. Practice role-playing to show how a teen can react to nasty remarks or bullies. Demonstrate how to ignore bad behavior. Challenge a teen to stay calm by counting silently to ten or walking away. With practice, teenagers can grow stronger and more confident, regardless of what type of painful situation they endure. The earlier you teach teens to speak up, walk away, or report negative behavior, the less likely that they will become victims. (See the "Practice Speaking Up" discussion in step 2 of part 1.)

In role-playing, you take on the role of the teen so you can demonstrate exactly how to respond to a given situation. Practice going through the situation several times and then switch places and let your teen try your role. To emphasize the importance of what you are trying to teach, get the whole family involved and let everyone try it.

Example

Carlos, age eleven, comes home angry and frustrated. He tells his mother that James always tries to hit him, and if he tries to run away, James chases him down. He admits he's scared and says he doesn't want to go back to school.

ADULT. Okay, Carlos, let's pretend I am you and you are James. Do exactly what James does and I will show you a different way to respond.

CARLOS. (*Puts on an angry face and pokes at the adult.*) Hey, you punk, you're stupid!

ADULT. (*Squares shoulders, puts up hands like a stop sign, looks "James" in the eye, and speaks up in a strong, calm voice.*) Stop it, or I will report you! (*Then, walks away with confidence.*)

Then switch roles and let your teen play the victim role. Try the role-play in several different styles, perhaps even doing it in funny voices one time. The idea is to practice so your teen will be more comfortable and confident when a real problem arises.

Note: If immature bullies are very aggressive, you may need to step in and talk to school authorities. If the problem continues to escalate, continue to speak up again but remember to do so without anger. Make sure that steps are taken to solve the problem. A meeting with parents and administrators may be necessary. Insist that violence should not be tolerated. Work with the school to make changes.

B. Evaluate a Teen's Maturity

You can tell a lot about a teen's maturity and ability to handle pain and anger if you follow some of these suggestions:

- *Ask questions.* "Why do you feel so angry?" Or say, "Explain what you mean." Dig deeper to find the problem.
- *Be patient.* Children will share how they feel if you listen without being judgmental.
- *Have a family meeting to discuss problems.* Let teens come up with ideas. Teens need to know you value their opinion and that they have family support.
- *Listen even if you disagree.* Encourage teens to find solutions. Ask, "What do you think is the best approach? What would you do differently?"

A good time to listen to children is just before they go to sleep. Teach children to say prayers, including what they've learned and why they are thankful. A child may ask to "Make Johnnie stop hitting" or "Make Mary give back my lunch money." Start listening when they are young, and they will discuss problems with you when they are older. But remember, as mentioned in step 1, even if you do not have a good track record for listening in the past, it's never too late to start.

Start *listening* to children at an early age.

Consider … The Listening Chair

Good communication starts in the family at an early age, but it is never too late to improve communication between parent and child.

Here is an easy way to develop great communication with younger children.

Set up a listening chair in your kitchen or family room. If children have a conflict at home, in the neighborhood, or at school, they often need to express their fears so they don't harbor anger or resentments. For example, if siblings are arguing, encourage them to share the problem in the listening chair. Or if your child is being bullied at school, he or she needs to talk, and you have the opportunity to find out what he or she is feeling.

The house rule can be if a child sits on the chair, family members need to stop what they are doing and listen to the child. Don't try to solve the problem, just listen! When the child is finished, ask thought-provoking questions, such as "What could you have done differently?" "How do you think this problem can be solved?" and "What are *you* going to do to make it better?"

When adults listen and let children solve their own problems, they are letting kids know they are capable and smart. You are helping to build their self-confidence and self-esteem.

Why is this important?

Children need to know they have a supportive family who listens!

1) When kids share problems, they don't grow up with anger or resentments but become empowered.
2) Don't solve problems but help children think through what *they* can do to solve a problem.

Why does this work? When families listen to each other, they reduce tension and kids learn they are capable, which gives them self-confidence.

Warning Signs

As teens mature, they often have trouble with relationships. When a teenager seems moody and out of sorts, that is the time to ask questions and listen. Try saying, "You seem distracted. Is there something you want to talk about?" or "Something seems to be bothering you. Can I help?" Regardless of what has happened, keep in mind you want to be a supporter and encourage teenagers to think for themselves. Avoid comments like "When I was your age …," "You ought to do …," and "If I were you …" Give them a chance to figure it out. Ask questions to help define the problem: "What made you feel that way? How did you handle it? What would you do differently?" Send the message that you know your teen is capable of sorting out problems and making decisions. Practice letting go of teenagers so they can find their identities and make responsible decisions.

A Life Experience

Karen Carpenter was a talented singer who died at a young age after years of struggling with anorexia. According to some accounts, she felt angry and frustrated because she had no control over her life. Her family, agents, and other people made all her decisions, and she didn't have the opportunity to work through her pain. The one aspect of her life that she felt she could control was her weight. Dieting became an obsession that eventually killed her.

Questions to Consider

Does everyone in the family show respect for one another? Do family members act in a mature, responsible manner? When you and members of the family say something in anger, do you apologize to one another?

C. Listen Carefully

If an adult criticizes your teen's behavior, don't get defensive. Listen! There may be a grain of truth in what he or she says, and you need to address it. Listen to family members, friends, neighbors, teachers, coaches, relatives, or police officers. They may not always be right, but they are sending you clues to help you raise a responsible teen, and you must be willing to listen. Ask questions of your teenagers to get their side of the story. Even good kids can lie to stay out of trouble. If you stop problems early, you will build a solid foundation for their future.

- An upset neighbor says, "Tommy was throwing rocks at my cat. Get him to stop it, or I will call the police." Have Tommy apologize, and let him know the consequences for cruelty to animals.
- A teacher says, "Jan doesn't listen or finish her work." Ask Jan what goes on in her classroom, perhaps saying, "What do you like or dislike at school?" If there is a problem, brainstorm with her and try to help Jan solve it. Work out an agreement about when she will sit quietly and do her homework. Stick to it. The agreement can only be changed if you both consent. Start regular study habits early.
- A friend says, "Joey is picking on my child." Listen to Joey. Often just a calm discussion can stop the behavior. Help Joey understand he needs to change his behavior, or there will be consequences.
- A family member says, "I'm concerned your older child is too angry with his little sister." Listen to your older child's point of view. Explain what behavior you expect. Anger can set up a negative pattern of behavior between siblings.

Ignoring bad behavior is a strong, silent statement of approval. Don't deny yourself the opportunity to "nip bad behavior in the bud." Problems don't just disappear; they can only get worse. Listen to others to prevent bigger problems in the future.

Besides listening to other adults, you must listen carefully to your children as well. If you hear one of them say, "I don't want to go to school," it may be a clue to a bigger problem. If you sense fear and anxiety, you should talk to the teacher. Consider working one day a week at the school or helping in the classroom. If school safety appears to be an issue, go to a school board meeting and find out what is being done. (If you can't attend meetings, find a relative or friend who can.)

Keep in mind you can't get all the facts in a few meetings. Get involved; ask teachers, students, and the janitor questions. When you have enough information, invite other parents to join you. Don't be overly critical, but offer recommendations for change and be available to help. Protecting children from violence or unsafe conditions should be everyone's priority. You can help other parents become aware of the need to get involved.

D. Awaken the Conscience to Help Teens Grow Stronger

Teenagers make errors in judgment. Use your power wisely. Be aware; you don't want to squash them so they rebel against *you*. However, you can't ignore problems. You want them to see their mistakes and make better choices in the future.

For example, Sean comes home with the smell of liquor on his breath, or his eyes tell you he has been taking drugs. You are sure he has taken something, but he swears he has not. What do you do? Here are several unreasonable possibilities for your response:

- scream and yell until he confesses
- take away all his privileges because he is a liar
- ignore it and hope you are wrong

Rather than following through on any of those options, consider this approach to handling problems so teens learn from the experience as you set a good example:

Instead of screaming, yelling, or ignoring the incident, use it as an opportunity to wake up a teenager's conscience. If the teen really is under the influence, state emphatically that you will discuss matters in the morning, and then do so. You *must* follow through even if that means you and the teen need to wake up early for the talk or that he will be late for school. If that happens, he must recognize being late as one of the consequences of his actions. State how you feel about drugs, sex, drinking, driving, and the related dangers. Let him know you love him but he needs to take charge of his own safety. Let him know how disappointed you would be if he had been drinking or on drugs. Reinforce the idea that you would be devastated if anything happened to him. Listen to his thoughts.

You can't be with him the next time he is tempted, but you can strengthen him with your support so he will make better decisions. Note—let teens know that if they are with anyone who is drinking, you will pick them up anytime or anyplace. (See the next section for more ideas on this issue.)

E. Don't Let Teens Avoid Pain through Drugs or Alcohol

Stay alert. Drug use starts at an early age. Lack of parental awareness about what a child is doing can lead to a painful future for the child and family. Drugs keep teens from maturing properly and make them vulnerable to inappropriate sexual activity, abuse, pregnancy, poor grades, low self-esteem, risky driving, violent behavior, and suicide. Get involved and get active to prevent drug and alcohol abuse before it takes over a child's life. In the following section, you'll see a few ideas for preventive steps. A parent must be aware of a teen's activities and calmly confront the dangers of drugs.

1. Prevent Substance Abuse: Set Up Agreements

Consider encouraging teens to sign an agreement to stay away from drugs. Not only can you elicit a commitment, but also discussing the agreement gives you an opportunity to really talk about the dangers of drug and alcohol misuse in a calm way. At an appropriate time, compose a written agreement together. *Parent and teen should both sign it.* Reassure teen that an agreement is not about lack of trust. It's a tool to help resist peer pressure and strengthen his or her commitment.

Drug Agreement (Sample)

I _____ promise I will not put myself in danger by taking drugs including alcohol. My _____ and I have discussed the dangers, and I know his/her concerns. As a family, we have discussed this issue. Also, I will call home and _____ has agreed to pick me up anytime or anyplace so I won't have to ride home with someone who has been drinking or taking drugs.

Signed:

_____   _____
Parent   Student

Beware! Agreements can be violated, so stay aware of your teen's activities and friends.

Author's Experience

A granddaughter told me that some teens will do drugs or drink regardless of whether they've signed an agreement. She felt they would not call for a ride home if the agreement was broken because the parents would get mad. Her suggestion for parents is to give teens a special ring to wear to remind them of how much their parents care. If a son or daughter is ever tempted, the ring can be a reminder to be strong and call home. The ring is a reminder that safety is the family's first priority.

2. Prevent Substance Abuse: Tap into a Higher Power

Religious involvement strengthens children so they can resist drugs and alcohol. Dr. William Miller's research at the University of New

Mexico shows that the risk for alcohol dependency is 60 percent higher among drinkers with no religious affiliation. Spiritual reengagement appears to be correlated with recovery. Addicts who work the twelve steps of Alcoholics Anonymous (which include a spiritual component) are more likely to remain abstinent than those who seek purely secular treatments. Dr. William R. Miller, Retired Professor of Psychology and Psychiatry – University of New Mexico. www.williamrmiller.net

3. Prevent Substance Abuse and Teen Suicide: Get the Facts

Educate yourself about drugs and alcohol abuse. Read, investigate, and research. To get you started, here are a couple of facts to keep in mind:

- The average amount of time between the beginning of drug use and parental discovery is about three years (Source: Operation PAR Inc. Break free of addiction – 1-888-727-6398).
- To find more information about drugs and alcohol go to www. Google.com - Type in, Commission on Substance Abuse to find local resources.
- Teenage suicide rates have tripled since 1960. The number of adolescents admitted to private psychiatric hospitals has increased fifteen fold during this period. (Source: Epidemiology of Youth Suicide and Suicidal Behavior Scottye J. Cash PhD and Jeffery A Bridge PhD https://www.ncbi.nlm. nih.gov/pmc/articles/PMC2885157/)
- In the last ten years, American deaths increased from 18,515 in 2007 to 70,237 people died in 2017 of opioid overdoses. Check out graphs on the Opioid Epidemic. Be aware of medications given to your family.
- (Source: www.opioid.thetruth.com).
- **Epidemiology of Youth Suicide and Suicidal Behavior**
- Scottye J. Cash PhD and Jeffery A Bridge PhD https://www. ncbi.nlm.nih.gov/pmc/articles/PMC2885157/

4. Prevent Substance Abuse: Know the Warning Signs

Helping teens turn to a higher power for support and creating a strong sense of community around them prevents self-destructive behavior. Teens may be experimenting because they are curious, or they may be trying to fit into the group. Or unintentionally, they may be trying to escape problems and pain they don't know how to handle. It is your job to find out what's going on. Ask questions and listen!

Beginning signs of self-destructive behavior may include smoking, using drugs, negative language, kicking a wall or punching a hole in a door, eating too much or too little, acting too sexy, becoming isolated, spreading harmful gossip about others, or blowing up for no reason. Or you may see a dramatic change in personality, such as withdrawing from peers, siblings, and parents; loss of energy; feelings of guilt or hopelessness; headaches; or stomachaches. These may be warning signs, and they won't just disappear. Ask questions and listen. Evaluate your teen's maturity. These issues should be approached calmly and with patience. Try to gather as much information as possible without jumping to conclusions. You may need to talk to his or her friends, teachers, or school counselor. Your goal is to stop destructive behavior before it gets out of control.

Signs of Substance Abuse

Drug use can become progressively self-destructive. You must be aware of your teen's behavior and these clues that can tell you if your teen is using drugs:

- the smell of alcohol or marijuana on breath or clothes
- change in friends
- change in attitude
- drop in school grades
- change in appearance
- problems involving police or the legal system

- selling of possessions or sudden appearance of new belongings
- disappearance of jewelry or household possessions
- finding drugs or drug paraphernalia
- emotional highs and lows, easily upset and generally unhappy
- making excuses for bad behavior, and everything is someone else's fault
- no motivation or interests

Parents' Enabling Behavior

As a parent, you love your teen, but without knowledgeable involvement, you may be helping your teen go down a self-destructive path. If you do not actively stand against drug and alcohol abuse, then you may be unconsciously supporting it. This approach is called enabling. In other words, even though you may not be giving a teenager drugs or alcohol directly, you may nevertheless enable him or her to be self-destructive. You will find some clues in the following list to help you recognize enabling behavior:

- denying and minimizing the teen's self-destructive behavior
- encouraging teens to drink at home
- allowing teens to attend parties with no supervision
- bailing a teen out of trouble at school, with police, or at court
- doing the teen's chores or other work for him or her
- letting your teen take advantage of you or other members of the family
- allowing the teen to manipulate you by caving in instead of enforcing rules
- giving money to an adolescent who is immature
- keeping peace at any price to avoid problems
- making excuses for inappropriate behavior
- expecting a teen on drugs to be rational
- ignoring the fact that addicts are persuasive liars
- trying to communicate with an out-of-control teen
- losing your temper or yelling and making threats

- allowing a teen to drive and continuing to pay for a car
- staying in denial, saying, "She'll or he'll outgrow it. It's only a phase."
- being unwilling to change your behavior
- avoiding educating yourself about the difference between drug treatment and therapy (Therapy cannot work until the teen is clean and sober.)
- losing your focus on a teen's behavior or not finding help when it's needed
- remaining ignorant about the signs of depression, which include tiredness or excessive energy, self-mutilation, stomachaches, headaches, frequent cough or respiratory problems, or sudden change in weight (gain or loss)

Find Help Immediately

If you see serious signs of drug or alcohol abuse, find help immediately. Contact a hotline, call your house of worship, look in the phonebook (under drug treatment), or call your doctor.

F. *Prevention*: Take Action to Protect Young People

Following are some ways you can be proactive in preventing teens' self-destructive behavior.

- Set up a "Listening Chair" at home when kids are young so they learn to share their concerns and feelings. (See: Part 2: Step 2)
- Help your teen grow stronger through involvement in positive activities. A teen can develop people skills by participating in programs focused on art, sports, cooking, crafts, and so on. Working with other people can teach leadership, teamwork, and cooperation.
- Do you have a drug-education program in your school? If not, get involved and find out what other schools are doing.

- If activities for teenagers don't exist, work with your local school, civic, or community group to help start a ball team, a music project, a dance group, and so on. "Idle hands are the devil's workshop."
- Gather support from friends and neighbors. Sign a petition. Your school and community will listen if you speak up without anger and are willing to help.

~~~

Use this space to jot down your thoughts about this step. Include positive action steps to empower youth.

Step 3

Handle Anger in a Positive Way

The greatest discovery of my generation is that human beings can alter their lives by altering their attitudes of mind.

—William James

Anger keeps teens confused, upset, and off-center. In step 3, your goal is to help them handle anger in a positive way. One method for doing that is to ask teens what they learn or feel when they become angry. You can also encourage teens to express their feelings without harboring resentment (see, "The Listening Chair," part 2, step 2). But remember, you will need to set the example. When you feel angry, don't let your anger spill over and pollute the thinking of children. Deal with your own issues of anger, and don't burden them with yours. Adults must work out their problems with one another without involving children, or the child may feel like he or she is the problem.

A. Defuse Family Fights

If you have a problem with a family member, don't discuss it with your teens. You don't want to divide the family into angry factions. It is the parents' job to pull all members of the family up, not knock one another down. You can't give teens the tools to handle the slings and arrows of life if you don't practice using them yourself. Anger issues need to be resolved so they don't fester into an "I am right; you are wrong" standoff.

When there is anger within the family, it may be due to poor communication or the parent's desire to control a teen's behavior rather than to provide guidance. Communication is a two-way street. It's not only what you say that matters but also what the teen hears. To reduce anger, ask the teen to repeat your instructions so you both know what's expected. Also, consider posting a bulletin board for family messages. Have each teen's chores written out on the board so they can be checked off when a job is complete. This organized approach can reduce misunderstandings and anger. If instructions are clear, it will be difficult for the teen to ignore them. Consequences should always be clear and obvious.

Another way to reduce angry confrontations is to give teens the opportunity to make decisions. Parents can defuse anger if they get a verbal agreement ahead of time.

For example, if you plan a party and need help cleaning up, cooking, or decorating the house, consider a verbal commitment. This commitment can reduce conflict and help get the job done. "Jason, everyone needs to pitch in and help. How much time can I count on you to help with this family project?" State what needs to be done and how much time you need from him, perhaps an hour. If he offers half an hour, you can compromise on forty-five minutes. When you negotiate an agreement, he feels that he is a valid part of the decision-making process and will be more likely to follow through without a hassle.

A critical component of reducing anger within families concerns discipline. Parents, stepparents, and guardians must decide together how they will discipline children. Agree on rules and boundaries before problems arise.

Agree too on spiritual training, and share information with one another. If teens feel they can play one parent against the other to get their way, they learn how to manipulate you, and this behavior can make your life difficult. Stand united when it comes to raising a child.

While it can be difficult, it is nevertheless important to minimize conflicts and anger between divorced spouses. For example, suppose your ex-husband promises to come to his son's birthday party. He doesn't show up. Your teen is devastated. How do you handle it?

There is a big temptation to let your anger take over. Do not give your teen any reason to hate his father or mother. Children have a strong spiritual bond with both parents regardless of behavior. Acknowledge your teen's disappointment, and wait for an explanation. Teens are smart. Don't tell them what to think. Let them know you are there to support and listen. Teaching your teen to be angry can set up a negative pattern of behavior.

B. Deliver Consistent Discipline

Set high standards when it comes to discipline. Discipline sets up specific consequences for misbehavior. Be firm and consistent. Follow through. Don't make empty threats, or children can soon learn how to manipulate you. Start at a young age.

Spanking may seem like an easy way to get a child's attention and may relieve your anger, but what are you teaching? This guide is about self-control. You can demonstrate self-control every day by your patience. You are your child's best teacher. Deal with problems without abusive punishment. You will need to stay calm under the most trying of circumstances. If you stay calm, teens learn from your self-control. If you are out of control, you become the problem, and teens will disregard *their* bad behavior.

A Life Experience

A mother slapped her daughter for swearing at her and calling her names. The daughter had a bruise on her cheek. She reported the incident to the school counselor. By law, the counselor had to report the *abuse* to the police. This case went to trial. The mother was acquitted, but the relationship between the mother and the daughter was damaged for years.

Questions to Consider

How do you handle discipline with your teen? Do you need to change in order for your teen to see that he or she needs to be more responsible and considerate of you?

To demonstrate how important it is to have a centered, balanced, and consistent approach to discipline, look at what The Sahm Community discovered "from the worst of the Parenting World." 12/10/2016

The Sahm Community states: "While we are all struggling with this parenting thing, it doesn't mean the world owes you anything. So at least be a decent human being – towards your family and other people. Short of child abuse and neglect, these are 10 of the worst things you can possibly do as a parent."

The ten worst things you can possibly do as a parent

- Giving unsolicited advise and judging other parents
- Helicopter parenting or hovering over your kids
- Not disciplining your kids
- Over scheduling your kids
- Requiring them to do physical labor too difficult for their age
- Not setting boundaries

- Take sports and academics way too seriously
- Setting to high expectations
- Over-sharing pictures of children on social media
- Seeing yourself as superior over single people or people without children

Additional information from the Sahm
Community: https://www.stayathomemommy.com/
my-kids/10-of-the-worst-things-you-can-possibly-do-as-a-parent/

Now here's a story illustrating a typical problem that arises in households with teenagers.

Example

Kim's high school friend arrived for a visit. The girls wanted to go bowling on a school night. At first, her mother said no, but Kim desperately wanted to go. She begged her mother to let them stay out until 9:30 p.m. Her mother said 9:00 p.m. They compromised on 9:15 p.m. At 9:15 p.m., the phone rang, and Kim begged to stay and play another game. Her mother said no and reminded Kim of their agreement. The girls arrived home after 10:00 p.m. Kim was angry with her mother because the game was a tie, and they wanted to break the tie. What would you do?

You have several options:

- ground her for a week
- scream and yell at her for disobeying the agreement
- threaten to send the teen someplace else to live
- stay calm to help your teenagers see their behavior

You can do all of the above, but why stress out? Restate the agreement clearly and how it was broken. State the consequences for not following the agreement, and stick to it. Go to bed. If you allow yourself to be drawn into an angry debate, your teen will not see that she was wrong. Teens need boundaries not just for themselves but also for your peace of mind. They must learn to be considerate of all members of the family. Teens struggle against boundaries, so expect resistance. If you stick with appropriate consequences for the infraction, they can learn to follow the rules. Remember, be consistent and handle anger in a positive way.

C. Take Action to Protect Young People

Adults can get to know neighborhood children. You are a possible mentor when you listen and help young people struggling with problems. Neighbors often help strengthen family support. When we care about others, we are setting an example for our children who are learning from us.

Some ideas to help struggling youth -

- Do you know of any young people who are in danger because of the angry people in their lives? Or do you know of any teens who are endangering others because of unresolved anger? Why not reach out informally to young people in trouble? Build a relationship with them slowly so they will feel led to trust and confide in you.
- Find out about anger-management courses in your community. Contact local police, health centers, or counselors for resources and information. Let young people know about these courses, and encourage them to participate.
- Check out conflict-management training for your school district. See if local schools would be willing to set up conflict managers on campus to help students resolve their problems.

~~~

Use this space to jot down your thoughts about this step. Include positive action steps you can use with your teenager.

Step 4

Find Your Center

The most important predictors of good health aren't diet and exercise—they are high self-esteem and good support. When we're comfortable with ourselves and can engage in meaningful relationships with others and a higher source, the natural healing mechanisms of the body function best. Your grandmother could have summed up the new molecular work in mind/body medicine with one word: love.

—Joan Borysenko, PhD
Author of *Minding the Body, Mending the Mind*

An immature teen can be easily influenced. That's one reason why it's important to help a teen find his or her center, which is the task you are taking on in step 4. Teens who are centered become stronger and will not feel the need to follow popular fads. Of course, teens want to be hip, but they must make good decisions for themselves. You don't want them to follow media stars because the trend is to smoke pot, drink, take drugs, have sex, get pierced, get tattoos, or have a baby. Your goal is to help teens become centered and strong enough to say no to behavior they know is wrong.

A Life Experience

A twenty-four-year-old disc jockey on a hip-hop radio station didn't like a new welcome sign erected in his community. Therefore, he urged his teen listeners to vandalize it. Over forty teenagers followed the disc jockey's directions and turned out for the caper. Several were arrested.

Questions to Consider

What other options could a disc jockey have suggested if residents didn't like the sign? What can parents do to make sure that radio personalities are responsible? Are pop stars, sports figures, or other celebrities exerting an undue influence on your teens? What can you do to reduce that influence?

A. Focus on Helping Teens Discover Their Spiritual Center

You cannot teach a teen to be centered if you are a bully or you're an overly sensitive pincushion type yourself. Do not allow abusive arguments to continue in front of a child. Settle major disagreements in private. You don't have to kiss and make up in front of children, but you do need to let them know that the relationship is still intact after you've made peace. You have to practice the behavior you want to see in your teen. If you are calm and respectful, your child will learn to mirror your behavior. Think before you speak.

Children have their own individual personalities from the day they are born. However, if a parent, stepparent, relative, or sibling bullies a child at home, the child is more likely to be a bully at school or the victim of a bully. This is a learned behavior. Your family must work to create a cooperative environment so every child can mature properly. You are your child's most important teacher. Start early.

Every teen is a unique challenge! Don't compare one teen with another. Each child grows at his or her own pace. Watch for clues so you can identify weaknesses that need to be strengthened. An aggressive child may act like a bully. An overly sensitive child can become the victim of a bully. It takes two individuals to have an abusive relationship. If one child is abusive and the other one tolerates it, they are both off-center. (See step 4 in part 1 for more on bullies, pincushions, and centered people.) Your teen will not be a victim or a bully if he or she learns to speak up with confidence and treats others with respect. Teens need adult support to find their centers so they won't get stuck in self-destructive relationships.

A Life Experience

A five-year-old girl was a little *bully*. An eight-year-old boy was teasing her by tossing her ball in the air. She stuck out her lower lip, grabbed him around the leg, and started hitting his kneecap. By comparison, her older sister was painfully shy, a "pincushion" child. She would have run home crying. Their mother had two different challenges raising her daughters. She would need to adapt her parenting skills for each child.

B. Set Boundaries to Help Teens Center

It is important for parents or guardians to set the ground rules at an early age so teens know their boundaries, limitations, and consequences. A teen who breaks the rules must be corrected immediately. If bad behavior is ignored, it can cause the family a great deal of pain in the future. Clear boundaries also help teens avoid bouncing from one extreme to the other, which, in turn, makes it easier for them to find and maintain their emotional centers.

These additional guidelines can help you in guiding teens and setting boundaries:

- Be a parent, not a best friend. A teen is not a best friend or confidant. Be careful not to share your problems with your teen. A teen may not be mature enough to handle your problems and his or her personal problems too. This added stress could make a teen depressed and resentful.

- Do not share your complaints about a relative or friend with any children. They may repeat comments without your knowledge. "My mother says you are too fat." "My daddy said your son is a spoiled brat." "I think your furniture is ugly." When any child makes inappropriate comments, adults know where the comments originated. Friendships and relationships can break down. You may not know what went wrong unless you ask.

- When teens are polite, they are respected and welcomed by others. Treat teens with respect, and they will treat others with respect. Respecting means listening to your teen and acknowledging anger without judgments and without put-downs.

- Teach good manners. When an adult is introduced, let teens know what you expect. Encourage children to stand up, have a firm handshake, smile, and look the other person in the eye. When you use *please* and *thank you* every day, your teens will know that manners are important. As you demonstrate good manners, your teen will follow your example. Role-play how you want your teen to answer the phone and the door. Good manners will benefit your teen. If your teen demonstrates respect for others, she or he is more likely to be given respect in return. (See step 2 in the part 2 for the discussion entitled "Practice Role-Playing to Strengthen Teens.")

- Admit when you are wrong and apologize. Teens need to know you are not perfect and can make mistakes. Apologize and ask them to forgive you. Being able to apologize is a strength, not a weakness. Teens are watching and learning from you. They are using you as their role model when relating to others.

Author's Experience

When I was six years old, I stole a small, shiny red-and-yellow box from a store. I presented it to my mother as a present when I got home. She asked me where I got it. I told her I found it on the store counter. We got back in the car and drove to the store so I could confess my misdeed to the store manager. I was petrified. I never stole anything again.

Questions to Consider

If your child took something that didn't belong to him or her, what would you do? What would your child learn if you ignored his or her bad behavior?

C. Nurture a Teen's Spirit

Spiritual knowledge is critical to a teen's understanding of him- or herself. A responsible religion helps a teen become centered and teaches him or her how to live by his or her own conscience. There are other benefits to religious training, including disciplining yourself to sit quietly, learning to listen to others, and recognizing the importance of study at an early age. Develop the habit of participating in religious instruction so you can help teach teens self-discipline and self-control, which will help them stay centered.

A Life Experience

Charles told his story. He was a bright student, second in his class at high school but always in trouble. A self-admitted bully, he stole from others, became violent, and took drugs. His mother, in a desperate attempt to change his behavior, said she would buy him a car if he graduated from high school. Charles, however, didn't care about education. He was angry with his mother for not marrying his father, and he didn't feel respected. He had watched *The Untouchables* on television and made up his mind to be a gangster and live the high life like Al Capone.

Charles's desire for respect became a nightmare. He sold drugs, became a drug addict, and remained one for twenty years. He was shot three times and spent seventeen years in prison. When I met Charles, he had been drug free and out of prison for nine years. He was working in construction and was a deacon at his church. One day a week, he counseled prisoners to help change their hearts. He told me, "I made my life a living hell. I just wish I had been smart enough to know how to live by God's Word when I was young instead of being a bully and hurting other people."

D. Help Teens Determine If They're Centered

The descriptions that follow present some of the qualities displayed by centered and socially aware teens. Check these descriptions against the behavior of your teens.

Centered teens can

- act independently and speak up with confidence while staying cool, calm, and collected
- talk about problems and look for solutions
- use self-control when upset and angry
- solve problems on their own
- look at problems as a learning experience
- When youth solve problems, they become more mature.

Socially aware teens

- care about others and use humor to overcome the rough times
- can be flexible and use communication effectively
- see the future as positive and a time to develop skills

E. Take Action to Protect Young People

- If you know of a neighborhood bully terrorizing other kids, investigate and see if you can talk calmly to the bully's parents and find out what's going on without blaming anyone. Perhaps you and a few other parents can work together with the family to turn things around.
- One of the best ways to get overly sensitive teens to take things less seriously is to encourage them to help others. Can you help teens set up a program to work with younger children in the neighborhood? Or can you check into volunteer activities in your community and get teens involved with you?

~~~

Use this space to jot down your thoughts about this step. Include positive action steps you can use with your teenager.

Step 5

Trust Your Instincts and Intuition

We are biologically programmed to respond to spiritual guidance—and I'm not talking about religion. It comes through intuitive hints about where we should go with our lives. The only way to have a truly creative and healthy life is to follow these inner promptings. Trust your gut and take risks.

—Christiane Northrup, MD
Author, *Women's Bodies, Women's Wisdom*

Encourage teens at an early age to use their intuition and instincts. When teens walk down the street, go to the park, or ride on bikes or in cars, they should be encouraged to use their instincts to stay safe. If they feel endangered at any time, they should know how to escape quickly. By teaching teens how to sense and avoid danger, you will not only be completing the work required in step 5, but you can also be helping to save lives.

A. Teach Teens Self-Protective Skills

All children, at the earliest age, should be encouraged to listen to their instincts. Do not frighten them, but let them know that it's okay to run away from an adult if they don't feel safe. And never force a child to kiss a relative or friend. Molesters usually know their victims. Let children decide which people they wish to embrace.

Teach them the "no, go, yell, tell" technique, which will increase their awareness and self-protective skills. This technique is adapted from guidelines developed by the Child Assault Prevention program.

1. No

Give young people permission to say no to an adult with confidence or to run away in an uncomfortable situation. Assure them that it is okay to leave immediately if anyone tries to entice them or threaten them. For the young, explain that no one should touch them in an area that is covered by a bathing suit because those areas are part of their personal, private space. Teens can also say no to unwanted contact on their bodies.

2. Go

Teach young people to get away from danger and run toward safety and help. Tell them to look for a well-lit area with people around, such as a store, restaurant, or gas station. They can run home, to a neighbor's house, or to a block parent. If you don't have a block parent in your neighborhood, start a program to keep all children in your area safe.

3. Yell

If your teen feels threatened, he or she must yell for help. You can teach your teen and your neighbors the special safety yell. This is a deep sound that signals other people that a child needs help.

How the Yell Works

The special safety yell is unique because it's only to be used when you are in trouble. It's a special yell because it has a special job—helping adults keep children safe. The yell has these distinguishing characteristics:

Low. It comes from the tummy, not the throat. It sounds deep, like a dog growling. But instead of making a *grrrr* noise, you make a low *huh* sound. The yell is different from the screech or screams you may hear as children play with friends. This yell lets adults know a child needs help immediately.

Loud. Take a very deep breath, and let your yell be the loudest it knows how to be. When you need help fast, you don't have time to be shy or polite.

Long. Because you take a deep breath, your yell can last a long time. Let it last as long as your breath lasts. Then take another deep breath, and do the yell again while you get away to safety and find someone who can help you.

The special safety yell says some very important things:

- The yell tells the person trying to hurt you, "I know what to do! I'm not an easy victim."
- The yell says to everyone within the sound of your voice, "I need help."
- The yell gets you going. It's the yell that breaks the spell. One of the easiest things to do when you are in danger is to freeze. It's also one of the worst things to do. When you take a deep breath, you are getting oxygen and energy to your brain and your muscles. That will help you figure out how to get away.

In Columbus, Ohio, where the Child Assault Prevention organization started, a girl gave the yell as an assailant dragged her toward his car. Five children in the neighborhood heard her and started doing their yells. Immediately, parents came running. The kidnapper let go of the girl and sped away.

4. Tell

Impress upon children that they must tell a parent, teacher, or other trusted adult if something bad happens to them—for example, if a stranger attempts to get them into a car or an older teen or adult attempts to molest them. Calmly explain they should tell even if someone warns them not to, threatens to hurt their family, or tells them they won't be believed or will lose their parents' love. Reassure children that they are loved unconditionally and they will never be blamed for something another person does, no matter what.

B. Use Role-Playing to Practice Self-Protection

As discussed in step 2 of the adult section of this guidebook, role-playing will help empower your teen. You play the role of the teen so you can demonstrate exactly what you want your child to do. Demonstrate several times, and then reverse roles and let him or her try it. Role-playing helps children respond in an appropriate manner to a particular situation. To emphasize the importance of what you are teaching, get the whole family involved and let everyone try it.

Use role-playing to teach street-safe techniques. Children are naturally intuitive, so encourage them to react immediately to an adult who may want to lure them away to a different place. For example, do a role-playing exercise to demonstrate what to do if a man drives up in a car and asks your child for directions or offers free video games or something cute like a puppy. You play the role of the child and run away immediately. Run in the direction the car came from or to trusted adults. A driver will seldom back up to chase a child.

Younger children should never be alone. Young children and even older ones should travel in a group or with an adult. All children should know how to react if they feel unsafe.

Children may not always obey parents, but they need to know what to do in an emergency in order to keep a bad situation from getting worse. Don't wait until something happens before you talk to children. Speak calmly about danger, and use role-playing to demonstrate safety techniques so they understand they have the power to stay safe.

Author's Experience

When I was ten years old, I went with my neighbor and her mother to Central Park in New York City to roller-skate. We were told not to skate in a wooded area called the Wilderness. We ignored our instructions and skated into the Wilderness. As we explored the area, we got confused about how to return. We crawled out on a ledge that overlooked the lake to get our bearings. As we figured out which way to go, we heard a noise behind us. We turned and saw a man standing behind us who exposed himself. We both jumped off the rock and pushed by him. Our fast actions took him by surprise, and we escaped.

The incident was reported to the police, and we lost our privileges. My mother was relieved we were safe but angry that we didn't follow instructions. I never went roller-skating in Central Park again. The dangers were explained to us, and I became more cautious.

C. Use These Tips to Increase Self-Protection

Encourage your teen to use these safety tips to increase his or her instincts for self-protection:

- Handle insults by speaking up to a bully and walking away. Learn to laugh at yourself (agree with the bully), but don't laugh at a bully. Stay calm, cool, and collected.

- Don't hesitate to walk or run away when you don't feel safe.
- Stay calm. Use self-control, and don't let your fear or anger come to the surface. Do not fight back unless you have no choice.
- Be creative in a dangerous situation, but think out your options. Consider doing the unexpected. Go limp, fall to the ground, and use your feet to kick. Say the unexpected, such as "My father will be here any minute," "I'm under a doctor's care for _____," or "I have a heart condition," and then grab your chest and faint. Do not allow yourself to be moved to another location. Yell and fight if you have no choice.
- To protect yourself from being moved to another location, do the unexpected. An attacker will expect you to struggle. Remember the vulnerable parts of the body; push fingers into the eyes, pull the ears, shove the palm of your hand upward to the nose, push your knee or foot to the groin, or stomp on the instep. Run like the wind to people or lighted areas.
- Your voice can be a powerful, self-protective tool. Use it. The special safety yell can often startle a bully or attacker into leaving. Or call out to a parent or an imaginary friend, "Hey, Dad, I'm over here. Help!" Yell "Fire!" to get attention if you need to.
- If you are concerned about your child's safety, consider having him or her take a self-defense course. This approach can help give a child additional self-defense tools and self-confidence.

Apply these street-safe guidelines to home computer use:

- Teach kids never to give out personal information, such as addresses, phone numbers, names, or names of schools to anyone on the Internet.
- Kids and teens should be taught never to give out family information, such as a credit card number or the name of their parents' employers.

- Teach kids never to agree to meet personally with someone they've contacted online.
- Teach kids not to answer any message that makes them feel uncomfortable.
- Teach kids that there are both good and bad places on the Internet.
- Put the computer in the family room or other public area rather than a bedroom.
- Review the logs of the sites your child has visited.
- Keep your password to the Internet a secret, and change it often.
- Set reasonable rules and guidelines for the times children can use the computer.
- Discuss rules and post them near the computer.
- Monitor compliance to rules, especially when it comes to the amount of time teens spend on the computer. A teenager's excessive use of online services, especially at night, may be a clue to a potential problem.
- Teach your teens how to interpret and evaluate the material that they see around them.

Author's Experience

I learned to use my instincts at an early age. I carried that experience with me into adulthood when I worked with the homeless in Oakland, California. Every Saturday, volunteers fed the homeless in the park. I had been helping a homeless man get his life together when he asked me to start a support group. I agreed to meet him and go to the corner church to discuss setting up a program with the pastor. I arrived at the appointed time, but my friend wasn't there. I waited, chatting with three women I had known for some time. Suddenly, they stopped talking and started to back away. I knew I was in trouble. I spun around, and an angry-looking man was coming toward me. He didn't respond as I jokingly asked if he had seen my friend. I didn't hesitate as I ran out of the park, waving goodbye.

D. Use Your Own Instincts

Use your instincts! Even a good teen will lie if he or she thinks it is a way to stay out of trouble. Be aware so you can catch problems early.

When my instincts told me something was wrong, I did a room check. It's okay to be a snoop. I was discreet and never let on what I found, but there were always clues, such as graded school papers I hadn't seen, notes from friends, pictures from parties, or drug paraphernalia. As a parent, I pay the bills, and I am responsible for my child. I want to be the first to know about problems, not the last.

Questions to Consider

What would you do if you discovered your child was taking drugs or drinking alcohol? How can you help teens get in touch with their self-protective instincts?

E. Take Action to Protect Young People

- Get involved. Find out if you can teach children how to discover their "center," and explain the no, go, yell, tell safety steps to preteens or teens at your local school or community center.
- Invite a local police officer or self-defense expert to present a demonstration on street-safe techniques to teens.

~~~

Use this space to jot down your thoughts about this step. Include positive action steps you can use with your teenager.

Step 6

Take Charge of Your Life

The harder the conflict, the more glorious the triumph.
What we obtain too cheap, we esteem too lightly.

—Thomas Paine

Throughout all the steps in this book, your teen is being encouraged to take charge of his or her life, whether that means building up self-esteem, as in step 1, or learning to turn anger into a positive force, the goal of step 3. Here in step 6, teens are given an opportunity to clearly declare their intentions to take responsibility for their lives.

As a parent or adult caregiver, a big part of your job is to let go somewhat so teens can take control of their lives. If you've laid the groundwork throughout their early years, they should be able to take on increased responsibility for themselves. If the process of maturation has been delayed, however, then you may need to move a bit more slowly. In either case, recognize that teens will make mistakes and that sometimes, it may seem as if they are taking one step forward and two steps back.

This push and pull toward maturity is normal. When babies are learning to walk, they stand and fall many times before they master the skill. So too will teens go through successes and failures before they reach a point of truly standing on their inner power. The best you can do as a parent is to help them get back on their feet when they slip and to stay out of the way when they are on the right path. In this adult portion of step 6, you will get ideas on how you can lead your family to take charge of an area that will help everyone become safer: home and neighborhood safety.

A. Take Charge of Home Security

Your home is your first line of defense in preventing crime. Here are a few tips to help you strengthen that line:

- Teach your teen how to handle home security: lock doors, lock windows, set alarms, and so on. Write down instructions if children are home alone. Keep emergency phone numbers handy, including that of a close neighbor. Talk to neighbors so children have permission to call them in an emergency or to run to their houses if they don't feel safe. Teaching young people these techniques will encourage them to be alert and to react quickly.
- Get every family member involved in home safety. If you remember to lock doors and windows and your children don't, your family is not safe. Consider taking a Sunday afternoon to give a lesson on home security. Ask family members to lock up the house and try to break in without doing any damage. You will be surprised how fast a small child can crawl through a pet door or find a downstairs window with a broken latch.

A Life Experience

Polly Klaas was kidnapped right out of her Petaluma, California, home. Polly and two friends were enjoying a slumber party. Richard Allen Davis crawled through an unlocked window while her mother and sister were sleeping in the next room. Twelve-year-old Polly was found murdered several days later.

B. Take Charge of Your Neighborhood to Keep Teens Safe

Young people should feel safe in their neighborhoods. If you don't feel safe, neither will your teen. Even if you feel safe, teens need to know their neighbors in case of an emergency. Talk with the people who live around you, and find out who is home during the day and who can be counted on in an emergency. You and your neighbors have a responsibility to create a safe environment for all children.

Here are some ways to make your neighborhood safer for your child:

- If you don't know your neighbors, consider inviting them over for a soft drink and cookies. Have a potluck, or, if you're ambitious, organize a block party. Get neighbors together so they can take charge of the neighborhood and deal with common problems.
- Take your teen on a walk through the neighborhood. Create a neighborhood-safety map to identify areas to avoid and places to go in an emergency. Have your teen draw the map with symbols to indicate safe areas as well as places to avoid.
- If you don't have a block parent program, go to your police department and find out how to start one in your neighborhood.
- Form a neighborhood child-safety committee. Together, neighbors can stop drug dealers and speeding cars. Or join forces to get the city to remove abandoned cars, fix potholes, and repair broken lights. Speak up without anger, and create a safe neighborhood. (For more information about creating a neighborhood-safety map, block parent program, and child-safety committee, check your local library for *Safe Homes, Safe Neighborhoods: Stopping Crime Where You Live* published by Nolo Press.)

A Life Experience

Wanda lived in a neighborhood that was changing. For two years, she saw teens selling drugs on the block. She called the police, but they said they couldn't do anything unless neighbors witnessed the transactions and agreed to testify in court. The problem escalated as fights erupted, and a bullet went through her car window. Wanda could see her property values going down as her fear went up. She called the neighbors together and, with the help of the police, organized a citizens' patrol. Neighbors jotted down descriptions, recorded license numbers, and photographed customers. Armed with this specific information provided by neighbors, the police made arrests. The neighbors learned to work together on a common goal, and the neighborhood became safe once again.

A Life Experience

I met Shirley Henke in 1970 when we were organizing the neighborhood-responsibility program in Orinda, California. She joined the volunteer committee because she was excited about helping people take charge of their own safety. As a former schoolteacher, she had organizing, writing, and people skills. She knew how to delegate, listen, and share ideas, and she never got upset. We coauthored *Alternative to Fear: Guidelines for Safer Neighborhoods, which helped launch the Neighborhood Watch program.* Our community had 17,500 residents, and with only ten volunteers working together, we reduced our crime problem by 48 percent without a local police department (Documented: Read guidebook, Alternative to Fear: Guidelines on www.safekidsnow.com). The community-wide program would not have been a success without the collaboration of ten committed volunteers working together for community change.

C. Take Action to Protect Young People

- Perhaps you've improved on your own home security, but what about that of your neighbors? Perhaps you can organize a safety day to help neighbors tighten up their own security and learn the importance of such things as locking garage doors.
- Do you have the facts from the police department on your neighborhood crime statistics? Does your town have a crime-prevention officer? Contact the police department for information and resources to make your neighborhood more secure.

~~~

Use this space to jot down your thoughts about this step. Include positive action steps you can use with your teenager.

Step 7

Set Goals to Succeed

> I respect the man who knows what he wishes. The greatest part of all the mischief in the world arises from the fact that men do not sufficiently understand their own aims. They have undertaken to build a tower, and spend no more labor on the foundation than would be necessary to erect a hut.

> —Johann Wolfgang von Goethe

Parents can help teens excel and become more secure by encouraging them to set goals. Working toward a goal builds a teen's self-esteem, and that is one of the underlying aims of step 7. Start with one or two small goals that can be accomplished easily. Then build up to longer-term goals so teens can gain confidence and learn perseverance.

A. Help Teens Set Goals

If your teen has completed the exercises for step 7 in part 1, he or she may have already identified a number of short-term goals. Perhaps you can review those goals to see whether they need to be stated in more detail or whether they should be broken down into smaller components. If your teen has not yet set any goals, here are some suggestions for projects he or she may want to take on:

- read one book from the library every month
- reduce a competitive swimming time by two seconds
- make beds or school lunch every day for a week without being told
- solve a disagreement by listening to each other without anger
- offer to help out around the house without being asked and do a good job
- raise a school grade by several points
- reach out and make friends with a new student or someone who doesn't seem to have many friends
- get involved in a project to help someone else
- spend half an hour each day learning a new skill

B. Acknowledge Accomplishments

Teens want parental approval, so give hugs when they fail and recognition when they succeed. Be creative in recognizing your teenager. If you think accomplishing a goal is a big deal, your teen will want to do more. Teens get a feeling of accomplishment if they see themselves making progress. Make it a habit to champion teens, and they will start setting goals on their own. Ideas to acknowledge your teen's accomplishments may include the following:

- put up a bulletin board to post reports and other achievements
- use magnets on the refrigerator to display reports, and add your own gold stars
- make your teen's favorite dinner
- invite your extended family or supportive friends to a celebration so everyone can cheer your child on

C. Take Action to Protect Young People

- Contact a local community college, business association, or professional group, and ask if there is someone who can speak to teens about goal setting and motivation.
- Help set up an awards dinner or celebration party for a group of teens who have accomplished some of their goals to become more street safe.

~~~

Use this space to jot down your thoughts about this step. Include positive action steps you can use with your teenager.

Step 8

Make Connections with Others

Turn off the television. Form warm relationships with family, friends, and relatives. And get involved in affairs of the community and country.

—Michael Jacobson
Center for Science in the Public Interest
Washington, DC

If you feel making connections with others is important, so will your teen, and that is your objective in step 8. All parents need support from neighbors, friends, a religious community, and relatives, but ultimately, the responsibility rests with parents and adult caregivers to raise strong, centered teens. Knowing neighbors and being involved in the local school, church, neighborhood, and community help all teens to feel more secure and to know that others care about them. (When people are connected, they need fewer laws and police. Citizen involvement can *prevent* crimes and other destructive behaviors.)

Stay alert. Don't let a teen get isolated from the family, school, or community. Teens need companionship and a sense of belonging so they can mature with the help of a caring environment. Social isolation is a danger sign. Items that promote isolation can include constantly using a smartphone, listening to too much music, texting, staying in their rooms, speaking only to a few friends, or overusing a computer or television. Young people need interaction with others to become self-aware and self-confident.

A. Build a Network of Support

Creating a safety net around teens may sound good, but it doesn't just happen overnight. You need to take the time and make the commitment to building relationships with a variety of people who can be a positive influence on your teen. This section offers some ideas to think about in making—and keeping—connections with others.

A Growing Problem

An AARP loneliness study published in 2010 reported that approximately 42.6 million US adults, age forty-five and older, were suffering from loneliness. "A 2018 Cigna survey indicates that Generation Z, adults between ages 18 and 22, may be the loneliest group of Americans." "Social isolation may rival obesity as a threat to people's healthy."

The Loneliness Effect – US News and World Report – September 2018 Barbara Sadlick – Contributor https://www.usnews. com/news/healthiest-communities/articles/2018-09-06/ loneliness-the-next-great-public-health-hazard

1. Maintain Family Connections

Family members (cousins, aunts, uncles, grandparents) can create a sense of balance by correcting and instructing children. Don't get defensive if they offer their opinions about your teen's behavior. You may need to hear what they have to say or at least balance the observations of others with your gut instinct about a teen's behavior.

Children and teens want to feel good about their families. It isn't expensive to create family memories and traditions. Plan a picnic, organize an outing with close relatives, go hiking, visit a farm or a park, bike on trails, or let your teen plan a party for family members. Be creative, and think of ways your teen can be involved in maintaining family connections.

Not all families, of course, have healthy relationships. You will have to make judgment calls about exposing your children to relatives who may be self-destructive or those who are abusing drugs, alcohol, or one another. Today, more than ever, families can get help.

Working together, a family can confront a person with an addiction. Once addicts realize what they are doing to other family members, they may seek treatment. Find local resources in your phonebook or call a hotline, doctor, minister, or rabbi.

Author's Experience

It took time to restore my family connections. When my first child was born, I began the healing process with my mother and invited her to visit. She still had a drinking problem, and I realized I couldn't change her behavior, but I could let go of my negative emotions and move on with my life. In order to be productive, I had to face my mother and come to the realization of what I could do and what I had no power to control. By my example, my children learned that they could accept other people even if they did not accept or support their behavior.

2. Get to Know Your Neighbors

If you know your neighbors, not only will your family be safer, but you will also be in a better position to handle problems that invariably arise with children and teens. Give neighbors permission to verbally correct your teen and call you if there are problems. You can stop bad behavior if you know about it.

Author's Experience

When I moved into a new neighborhood, I made it a point to meet my neighbors and ask them to call me if my children didn't behave. This effort proved to be a good investment of my time. I was the first to know if there were problems. Two boys in our neighborhood threw mud clods at a neighbor's stucco house. The neighbors spotted them, and everyone agreed. We scolded them, and the boys spent the next two hours cleaning up the mess that only took a few minutes to create. They never did that again.

Questions to Consider

Will your neighbors call you if your child misbehaves? Will you appreciate hearing that there is a problem that needs immediate attention?

Author's Experience

As a crime-prevention coordinator, I worked with neighbors who had a problem with a nine-year-old boy who was stealing from garages, bullying children, and smashing mailboxes. One father tried to talk to the boy's mother, but she slammed the door in his face. Another neighbor reported stolen tools and broken flowerpots to the police. The officer talked to the mother, but nothing improved. The neighbors had a meeting and documented all the problems. They appointed a group of the most tactful neighbors to approach the mother and offer assistance, without blaming her. The mother was upset and told the neighbors she was going through tough times. The whole neighborhood worked with the mother and her child. Now this grown-up young man attends college.

3. Connect to Others, Spiritually

Churches, temples, mosques, and other spiritual institutions give children tools for handling emotional development. Be involved in the faith of your choice, and make sure that the religious group you're involved with is teaching your teen how to grow strong and how to discover inner power. Religious instruction helps children learn self-discipline as they sit quietly and listen, which is good preparation for school and life. Sunday school and other religious instruction can teach children to be discerning so they will see the difference in behavior if they are mistreated. The vast majority of religious teachers volunteer because they love children. Children should have the same treatment in day care or school. If they don't have a caring environment, they are more likely to tell you.

Author's Experience

I was presenting a child-safety program at a high school when a welfare mother of a three-year-old said her son was coming home from day care with bruises. She *was* worried because he was becoming easily intimidated and he didn't like his teacher. I suggested she talk to the teacher and discuss the bruises. If she was satisfied with the explanation, she could accept the teacher as a partner in raising her child. Her interest would send a message of concern and let the teacher know she was paying attention. Be discreet, and talk to other parents and children. Make surprise visits to the center. If necessary, discuss concerns with the director. If all else fails and you are still convinced something is wrong, remove your child immediately and report it to social services. This same advice can be adapted to other situations regardless of a child's age. Investigate the facts, build partnerships with others, teach children to speak up and protect themselves, and ultimately, if necessary, remove them from the day-care center.

B. Turn Negative Encounters into Positive Ones

When you make connections with others, not every encounter will turn out well. But it's up to you to find ways to turn a negative into a positive experience. Don't let one bad experience pull you down. Find other people to support you and your family. You may have to search. If teens see you overcoming obstacles, they will learn to do it too.

Author's Experience

My husband, our young daughter, and I moved into an upstairs apartment. Since no one came to welcome us, I decided to take my daughter outside to the swing set and see if anyone would say hello. Within a few minutes, the downstairs neighbor, who had two young daughters, opened her door and screamed, "Get that kid off my swing set!" I apologized, but I wasn't happy about my unfriendly neighbor. This became a challenge as I went door-to-door, introducing my two-year-old daughter and myself. Other neighbors were friendly, and I made good friends. I felt sorry for the children downstairs because their mother kept them isolated from other children.

C. Take Action to Protect Young People

- Get involved in your child's school. Find out the school-safety record. What problems exist? You won't get the whole picture at one or two meetings. Ask questions of teachers and students. Serve on the PTA, or run for the school board to help improve your teen's school and broaden your network of support.
- Help organize social events that bring teens together with people they may not otherwise meet. You can set up visits with seniors or a charity event. Or nominate teens to serve as youth representatives on local neighborhood councils or community groups.

D. What city leaders can do to reduce crime and gun violence!

Gun Violence: A Mental Health Crisis for Youth – Video, Hosted by Ted Koppel with guest speakers – Students speak up

https://www.aspenideas.org/session/
gun-violence-mental-health-crisis-youth

There is a great deal of concern about the mental health of families and youth who are exposed to violence. City leaders can hire and train **"Neighborhood Safety Experts"** to help bring citizens together to create safer neighborhoods. Safety Experts need to look like and speak the language of the community.

For benefits and information, check out:

https://safekidsnow.com/wp-content/uploads/2018/11/Why-City-Leaders-Need-NSE.pdf

SPEAK UP and TAKE ACTION if you are concerned about crime and violence! Set up a meeting with local leaders. They can ignore one or two people but they can't ignore ten or more like-minded friends and neighbors wanting their leaders to take action to stop crime and violence.

Together, "we the people" have the power to create change in our homes. Neighborhoods and communities.

~~~

Use this space to jot down your thoughts about this step. Include positive action steps you and/or teen can use with your teenager.

Step 9

Find Your Inner Power

Be the change you wish to see in the world.

—Mahatma Gandhi

Most parents use external control (rules, boundaries, and limitations) to teach teens important self-control lessons. If a teen disobeys, there are consequences, such as being grounded or losing privileges. If teens get out of control, the police and school officials use laws, curfews, community service, teen courts, and suspension or school detention. The last resort is the juvenile justice system, which includes juvenile court, juvenile hall, and the state youth authority. These external controls can turn a teen around, but they have limitations.

Step 9 is designed to help teens learn that true power comes from within. An individual who doesn't feel he or she has any power can rebel against parents, friends, loved ones, or society. Adults will save themselves a lot of grief if they work together, show respect for others, and give teens guidance in living by spiritual laws. When adults show this kind of leadership, teens can develop the internal controls that help them become self-aware, self-disciplined, and self-directed. A spiritual understanding of self can help teens find inner power and be empowered and keep them street safe.

A. Guide Teens around Obstacles

For teens to find their true power, they will need to overcome obstacles that block their path to the healthy expression of who they really are. One block is the inability to forgive others. Another crucial block to overcome is the recognition of the dark side of power—evil—that is the misuse of the spiritual gifts given by the Creator. This section discusses both of those obstacles.

1. Explain the Importance of Forgiveness

Teens need to understand the power of forgiveness and practice forgiving others for their own sake. Victims must also find ways to forgive others so they don't end up destroying themselves. If something bad happens, find immediate help. If a teen fills his or her mind with anger, greed, selfishness, and vengeance, he or she will become isolated and off-center. Instead of finding inner power, teens will become weak and obsessive, as these life-experience stories illustrate:

A Life Experience

Ted Kaczynski, known as the Unabomber, killed two people and injured twenty-three with mail bombs. He accused his parents of "ruining his life." Kaczynski wrote his parents, saying, "I can't wait until you die so I can spit on your corpse." He told his brother, "I have a good deal of anger in me, and there are lots of people I'd like to hurt." He hurt other people and destroyed his own life.

A Life Experience

Two teenage sisters were walking home from school when two men kidnapped them. They raped the girls and threw them off a bridge. The younger sister died in the icy water, while the older sister's fall was broken when she hit a support beam. Although she was severely injured, she made it to shore. According to her family, she never learned how to handle the devastating trauma. Fifteen years later, she committed suicide by jumping off the same bridge.

2. Expose the Dark Side of Power

There is the potential for good or evil within each of us. We have the power to make choices about the path we follow. Some individuals have so much pain and anger they gradually shut down their consciences. They no longer feel the pain they cause. We call this state feeling no remorse. When the conscience is shut down, humans are capable of horrendous acts of violence. There is plenty of evidence that evil, or the dark side of humanity, has increased. Terrorism, assaults, stalking, racism, hate groups, road rage, gangs, random violence, abuse, rapes, and murders are obvious examples of the behavior of individuals who haven't learned they have the inner power to change. These people are spiritually ignorant and influenced by media replays, which can lead to copycat violence. They never developed their own identities. They misuse their inner power and direct it at controlling the lives of others. Murder is the ultimate evil power. Evil behavior is now showing up at all age levels.

A Life Experience

Thirty-nine members of the Heaven's Gate cult committed suicide in March of 1997. Their leader gained control over all members. Spiritually immature, dependent, sensitive young people gave away their power to a cult leader.

B. Help Teens Discover Their Inner Power

It is a parent's responsibility to help teens find their center so they can learn to live by the dictates of a healthy conscience. (See step 4 in part 1.) The most important connection you can help your teen discover is a connection with the Creator. When you help children understand spiritual laws, you are protecting them from a confusing world. All teenagers need to know they have inner power to change their behavior and live a productive life.

A religious organization or spiritual fellowship can help you teach your teen the benefits of internal control. Your teen can also learn to handle emotional problems. As children grow stronger, they begin to see they have the power to overcome any obstacles.

A Life Experience

An alcoholic father verbally abused his wife and two boys. He sat on the church steps and cursed the parishioners every Sunday morning. His family prayed for him. One day, after his wife told him he reeked of alcohol, he felt dirty. After taking a shower, he still didn't feel clean. He looked in the mirror and had a spiritual awakening as he saw the truth about himself. He fell on his knees, made a commitment to serve, and asked for forgiveness. Within three years, he became the pastor of the same church where he had cursed the parishioners.

A Life Experience

A friend was diagnosed with terminal cancer and given only a few months to live. As a high school teacher of many years, he rediscovered his inner wisdom and belief that anyone can improve his or her way of thinking and health to achieve happiness. He changed his lifestyle, changed his diet, and renewed his faith. He lived another twelve years after his terminal diagnosis.

Author's Experience

Years ago, I attended a variety of churches and found that some churches were doing little to help the larger community. I was concerned about my children growing up in a society that lacked concern for others. I felt there were too many angry people divided along racial, religious, and economic lines. It seemed ordinary people like me didn't know what to do or how to help. I started praying and made three requests: (1) My husband and I had two wonderful daughters, and I was pregnant. I asked God for a baby boy. (2) I acknowledged I hadn't done well in school, so I didn't want to do any extensive reading or writing. (3) I didn't want to do any public speaking. Otherwise, I asked, "What can I do to serve?"

That night, I couldn't sleep. I remembered my grandmother used to tell me, if you want answers and you have a sincere heart, take time to identify your concern and point at random to a page in the Bible. When I opened my eyes, I read, "And Ur brought forth a son and called him Abraham." I stared in disbelief. Did it mean I was going to have a baby boy? I read the line over and over again. Was it a sign?

I spent two more days in meditation. I had so many ideas I started jotting them down. Some ideas included conducting a community-education series at the local high school, forming a group consisting of police officers and neighbors who could work together on neighborhood issues, setting up interviews with former drug addicts to help wake up high school students, and establishing neighborhood-protection committees to regain a sense of community.

My assignment was a tall order. However, before my son turned three, I had accomplished all these goals in my community with the help of many dedicated community leaders and citizens.

Teens should know that God doesn't always respond to prayers by just giving us what we want. I did have a son, but I also set up conditions in my prayer, asking that I not be required to do a great deal of reading, writing, or public speaking. Now, after thirty-nine years as a community crime and violence prevention consultant, I can tell you I've done more than my share of reading, writing, and public speaking! Sometimes, our prayer becomes "not my will, but thy will."

C. Take Action to Protect Young People

- Discuss with teens the source of their inner power. Encourage them to read, study, question, and participate in a religious or spiritual practice.
- Instead of rejecting teens who look different or who may be involved in dangerous activities, do what you can to reach out to them. Give them information and a safe place to communicate to help expose the cults, celebrities, or other leaders who misuse power and exploit teens for their own gain.

~~~

Use this space to jot down your thoughts about this step. Include positive action steps you can use with your teenager.

Step 10

Discover Your Unlimited Potential

Meditate 15 minutes twice a day. It will help you gain an infinite storehouse of knowledge, energy, and bliss. It requires no lifestyle changes, but as you continue to evolve, you may find that unhealthy habits start to naturally fall away.

—Deepak Chopra, MD
Author, *The Seven Spiritual Laws of Success*

Helping teens discover their unlimited potential should be the mission of all parents and adults who care about them. Adults can guide a teen's destiny by creating networks of support, teaching self-discipline, correcting bad behavior, setting up fair rules to follow, and teaching young people how to handle anger and pain. As you set an example and show unconditional love, your teen will grow strong and self-confident. You don't have control over the path a teen ultimately decides to take, but you can help the teen make good decisions for the future. Step 10 is designed to give you ideas for helping teens fulfill their special destinies.

A. Encourage Teens to Share Their Dreams

Do you know what your teen hopes to do in the future? Do you know the dreams he or she is too shy to tell anyone else about? By offering a sympathetic ear and a nonthreatening environment, you can open the lines of communication that allow teens to tell you about their secret hopes and desires. Encourage teens to share their dreams with you. Then support them by giving them books, information, and other forms of support to help them make those dreams come true.

B. Broaden Teens' Horizons

One way to help teens discover their unlimited potential is to broaden their horizons by showing them different corners of the world. Wherever you live, it's important to take teens to different neighborhoods so that they learn about others. Don't wait to be invited; just go and see what is going on. Teens should experience variety so they can make comparisons.

Author's Experience

My husband was out of town on Mother's Day. I decided to take my eleven-year-old son to church in San Francisco. The congregation was a multicultural group in a wide variety of fashions. The service was long, and my son was uncomfortable as everyone held hands singing and swaying to the high-energy music. It was loud and fun, but he would have none of it. He sat in the pew and sulked. When the service was over, he dashed for the exit. He was just in time to be scooped up in the long black cape of the pastor. He struggled to free himself and darted out the door. I found him waiting around the corner. He was angry and exclaimed, "Why didn't you warn me?" I brushed it off as a learning experience. I forgot all about our trip until the following Mother's Day. My son proudly announced he had saved his money. I was shocked yet pleased when he said he was taking me to church in San Francisco.

C. Take Action to Protect Young People

- Share your experiences. Everyone has some talent and knowledge that can benefit a young person. Volunteer to be a speaker at your local high school's career day or invite teens to visit your workplace. If you're not involved in a career, explore other ways to share your expertise, such as writing about your experiences in the local paper or presenting a class demonstrating your special hobby. However you do it, your goal is to give of yourself so that teens can discover their potential.

- Challenge teens to stretch their limits. Help develop projects that ask teens to go beyond their ordinary limits and thinking. For instance, if a group of teens plans to raise $500 through a charity run, encourage them to set a goal of $1,000 instead. Or challenge them to gather a few thousand signatures on a petition to improve the community. By going further than anyone thinks possible, teens learn they can tap their inner power to realize their dreams.

~~~

Use this space to jot down your thoughts about this step. Include positive action steps you can use with your teenager.

Review

Empowerment Tips for Parents and Adults

The following are suggestions can help keep families and youth safe:

- Set boundaries, rules, and reasonable consequences for unacceptable behavior.
- Don't allow any unacceptable or violent behavior at home.
- Evaluate your child's maturity and progress…often.
- Have age-appropriate consequences for bad behavior, and be consistent.
- Help your child learn how to handle his or her emotions and stay centered.
- Encourage your child to trust and listen to his or her conscience, instincts, and intuition.
- Role-play and practice street safety; teach the "no, go, yell, tell" technique.
- Learn the signs of bullying, the cycle of abuse and substance abuse.
- Teach your child how to stay safe at home, in the neighborhood and on the computer.

- Listen to people who offer correction of your child to help him or her succeed.
- Be a role model. Get involved in your child's school and your neighborhood.
- Encourage teens to get involved in activities that challenge them.
- Create a supportive environment at home and in the neighborhood.
- Create a network of caring people around your child, including family, extended family, friends, and neighbors. A spiritual or religious community can help empower your child.
- Be the example of how you want your children to behave.
- Be a peacemaker at home, in your neighborhood and the community!

It takes healthy relationships with families and neighbors working together to create a safety network around children. Every child deserves a safe home and neighborhood.

YOU have the power to create a safe home and neighborhood for your children and the children living around you! Make it happen!!

For more information: www.safekidsnow.com

Resource List

Self-Help for Teens

The Survival Guide to Bullying: Written by a Teen by Aija Mayrock
    (written by a teen for teens)
The 7 Habits of Highly Effective Teens Workbook by Sean Covey

Resources for Adults

Brainstorm: The Power and Purpose of the Teenage Brain by Dr.
    Daniel Siegel
*The Spiritual Child: The New Science on Parenting for Health and
    Lifelong Thriving* by Lisa Miller, PhD
The 7 Habits of Happy Kids by Sean Covey
Raising Self-Reliant Children in a Self-Indulgent World by H. Stephen
    Glenn, PhD, and Jane Nelsen, EdD
The Intuitive Parent: Why the Best Thing for Your Child Is You by
    Dr. Steve Camarata
*Bullied: What Every Parent, Teacher, and Kid Needs to Know about
    Ending the Cycle of Fear* by Carrie Goldman
The Teenage Brain by Dr. Frances E. Jensen
*The Conscious Parent: Transforming Ourselves, Empowering Our
    Children* by Shefali Tsabary, PhD
Helping Your Kids Cope with Divorce by M. Gary Neumann, LMHC

Siblings without Rivalry and *How to Talk to Kids so Kids Will Listen and Listen so Kids Will Talk* by Adele Faber and Elaine Mazlish
Stop Depriving the World of You: A guide to getting UNSTUCK
By Darlene M. Corbett
Positive Discipline by Jane Nelsen, EdD

Websites

Safe Kids Now (resources, books, and programs)
    www.safekidsnow.com
Discovery Education (parent education to help your student)
    www.discoveryeducation.com
"Parenting Guide to Internet Safety"
    www.fbi.org
Drugs and Youth: National Council on Alcoholism and Drug Dependency
    www.ncadd.org
Office of Justice Programs
    www.ncjrs.gov
Office of Juvenile Justice and Delinquency Prevention
    www.ojp.gov
The Children's Partnership
    www.childrenspartnership.org
"Parents' Guide to Internet Safety"
    www.fbi.gov
Information and Stats about Youth
    www.kidsdata.org